EXPLORE

A 21-DAY JOURNEY TO KNOWING JESUS

Copyright 2016 – Craig Etheredge. All rights reserved.

Published by **discipleFIRST**
5405 Pleasant Run, Colleyville, TX 76034

Unless otherwise noted, scripture quotations are taken from the Holy Bible, New Living Translation, copyright ©1996, 2004, 2007, 2013, 2015 by Tyndale House Foundation. Used by permission of Tyndale House Publishers, Inc., Carol Stream, Illinois 60188. All rights reserved.

ISBN: 978-0-9993439-0-6
PRINTED IN THE UNITED STATES OF AMERICA

Book Design and Layout: Kim Slater - katCreative.net

EXPLORE

A 21-day Journey to Knowing Jesus

verb ex·plore \ik-'splor\
- to look at (something) in a careful way to learn more about it: to study or analyze (something)
- to talk or think about (something) in a thoughtful and detailed way
- to learn about (something) by trying it

Welcome to the chance of a lifetime. You are standing on the brink of a 21-day journey that will lead you to encounter and experience the most powerful and influential person who ever lived – Jesus Christ. There are many opinions about Jesus circling around and, over the years, people have painted Him differently. Some see Jesus as a spiritual guru sharing tidbits of wisdom and "words to live by," all while holding a double mocha decaf latte. Others see Jesus as a stained glass religious icon who lived thousands of years ago, but has no real relevance today. Still other people see Jesus as a good person who was misunderstood in His day and still misunderstood today. How do you see Jesus? More importantly, how did the people who knew Him the best see Him?

In the pages that follow you are going to read an ancient document written by one of Jesus' closest friends. His name is John. He was one of the first men to follow Jesus. Later John became one of Jesus' inner-circle leaders and saw firsthand many of Jesus' miracles. More than a distant follower or face in the crowd, John was very close to Jesus. He was so close that when Jesus was dying on the cross, He turned to John and commissioned him to take care of His mother, Mary. Needless to say, Jesus trusted John implicitly. John was the first one to see the empty tomb of Jesus. John was one of the first to see Jesus alive again after His death. John witnessed firsthand Jesus ascending to Heaven. Ultimately, John became a part of the leadership team who spread the message about Jesus all around the world. In his later years, John emerged as a senior leader in one of the most influential churches in Asia, the church of ancient Ephesus. If anyone knew Jesus, it was John. In his twilight years, John sat down to write out some of his firsthand accounts of Jesus' life and ministry, and he wrote those words so that people like you and I could read them and explore the real Jesus – the Jesus he knew and the Jesus he followed. John writes, "*...these are written so that you may continue to believe that Jesus is the Messiah, the Son of God, and that* *by believing in him you will have life by the power of his name,"* **(John 20.31 NLT)**.

Over the next 21 days you will read the firsthand, eye-witness account of John. Along the way, you will explore Jesus himself and discover who He is and how He can change your life today. But before you begin, let me give you a few pointers to help you along the way. First, I encourage you to read one chapter a day for the next 21 days. If you do this, then you will catch the flow of John's story of Jesus. Leaving big time gaps between readings may cause you to forget what John said previously and miss the full impact of his message. Second, embedded in each reading are a few questions and clarifications. I have added helpful information to clarify for you what John is saying, and the questions are crafted to help you to focus on the main points of his story. Take time to read the clarifying points and answer the questions. Third, as you read John's account you will discover that the sentences or phrases are actually numbered. These numbers were not put there by John in his original writing, but were added later to make it easier to study what John wrote. These numbered sentences or phrases are called *"verses."* Occasionally I will ask you a question that pertains to a specific verse. Just look up the verse number and read that sentence. It's pretty easy! Fourth, I encourage you to gather once a week with a group of people to discuss what you have read. As you talk about what you are learning, you will sharpen your thoughts and gain insights from others.

You are standing at the beginning of a wonderful journey. What if this exploration really changes your life? What if you really come to experience Jesus in a real and personal way? Think about the difference He could make in your life now, and certainly in your life beyond the grave. **It's time to explore, so let's get started!**

DAY ONE

John 1.1-51 (NLT)

Your journey begins with an introduction. If I wanted to introduce someone to you, I might use different titles to describe him. For example, I might say, *"This is my dad,"* or, *"This man was my professor when I was in college,"* or even, *"This man is my best friend."* All three titles, "dad," "professor," "best friend", are different words I could use to describe a person. In fact, all three titles could be used to describe the same person! In this reading, John is going to introduce Jesus to you, and he is going describe Him using various titles. These titles were very clear to the first-century Jewish person, but have been lost in our time and culture, so I'll provide some brief explanations. This reading describes how John and many others first met Jesus. So, get ready to meet Jesus!

Prologue: Christ, the Eternal Word

¹*In the beginning the Word already existed.*
The Word was with God,
and the Word was God.

²*He existed in the beginning with God.*

³*God created everything through him,*
and nothing was created except through him.

JESUS: THE WORD

A word is a sound or symbol that expresses a meaning. In the same way, Jesus expresses to us who God is and what He is like. In fact, you could just replace the phrase *"the Word"* with the name Jesus and this section would be perfectly clear.

4The Word gave life to everything that was created,
 and his life brought light to everyone.

5The light shines in the darkness,
 and the darkness can never extinguish it.

6God sent a man, John the Baptist, **7**to tell about the light so that everyone might believe because of his testimony. **8**John himself was not the light; he was simply a witness to tell about the light. **9**The one who is the true light, who gives light to everyone, was coming into the world.

10He came into the very world he created, but the world didn't recognize him. **11**He came to his own people, and even they rejected him. **12**But to all who believed him and accepted him, he gave the right to become children of God. **13**They are reborn—not with a physical birth resulting from human passion or plan, but a birth that comes from God.

14So the Word became human and made his home among us. He was full of unfailing love and faithfulness. And we have seen his glory, the glory of the Father's one and only Son.

15John testified about him when he shouted to the crowds, "This is the one I was talking about when I said, 'Someone is coming after me who is far greater than I am, for he existed long before me.'"

16From his abundance we have all received one gracious blessing after another. **17**For the law was given through Moses, but God's unfailing love and faithfulness came through Jesus Christ. **18**No one has ever seen God. But the unique One, who is himself God, is near to the Father's heart. He has revealed God to us.

The Testimony of John the Baptist

19This was John's testimony when the Jewish leaders sent priests and

Temple assistants from Jerusalem to ask John, "Who are you?" [20]He came right out and said, "I am not the Messiah."

[21]"Well then, who are you?" they asked. "Are you Elijah?"

"No," he replied.

"Are you the Prophet we are expecting?"

"No."

[22]"Then who are you? We need an answer for those who sent us. What do you have to say about yourself?"

[23]John replied in the words of the prophet Isaiah:

"I am a voice shouting in the wilderness,

'Clear the way for the Lord's coming!'"

[24]Then the Pharisees who had been sent [25]asked him, "If you aren't the Messiah or Elijah or the Prophet, what right do you have to baptize?"

[26]John told them, "I baptize with water, but right here in the crowd is someone you do not recognize. [27]Though his ministry follows mine, I'm not even worthy to be his slave and untie the straps of his sandal."

[28]This encounter took place in Bethany, an area east of the Jordan River, where John was baptizing.

Jesus, the Lamb of God

[29]The next day John saw Jesus coming toward him and said, "Look! The Lamb of God who takes away the sin of the world! [30]He is the one I was talking about when I said, 'A man is coming after me who is far greater than I am, for he existed long before me.' [31]I did not recognize him as the Messiah, but I have been baptizing with water so that he might be revealed to Israel."

[32]Then John testified, "I saw the Holy Spirit descending like a dove from heaven and resting upon him. [33]I didn't know he was the one, but when God sent me to baptize with water, he told me, 'The one on whom you see the Spirit descend and rest is the one who will

baptize with the Holy Spirit.' **34**I saw this happen to Jesus, so I testify that he is the Chosen One of God."

JESUS: THE LAMB

The Jewish people often sacrificed lambs and goats at the temple for the forgiveness of their sins. The innocent paid the penalty for the sins of the guilty. The phrase, *"scapegoat"* is taken from this practice. Here Jesus is called the *"Lamb of God,"* meaning that He is the ultimate scapegoat, the one who can take away our sins once and for all.

The First Disciples

35The following day John was again standing with two of his disciples. **36**As Jesus walked by, John looked at him and declared, "Look! There is the Lamb of God!" **37**When John's two disciples heard this, they followed Jesus.

38Jesus looked around and saw them following. "What do you want?" he asked them.

They replied, "Rabbi" (which means "Teacher"), "where are you staying?"

39"Come and see," he said. It was about four o'clock in the afternoon when they went with him to the place where he was staying, and they remained with him the rest of the day.

40Andrew, Simon Peter's brother, was one of these men who heard what John said and then followed Jesus.

41Andrew went to find his brother, Simon, and told him, "We have found the Messiah" (which means "Christ").

42Then Andrew brought Simon to meet Jesus. Looking intently at Simon, Jesus said, "Your name is Simon, son of John—but you will be called Cephas" (which means "Peter").

43The next day Jesus decided to go to Galilee. He found Philip and said to him, "Come, follow me." **44**Philip was from Bethsaida, Andrew and Peter's hometown.

45Philip went to look for Nathanael and told him, "We have found the very person Moses and the prophets wrote about! His name is Jesus, the son of Joseph from Nazareth."

46"Nazareth!" exclaimed Nathanael. "Can anything good come from Nazareth?"

"Come and see for yourself," Philip replied.

47As they approached, Jesus said, "Now here is a genuine son of Israel—a man of complete integrity."

48"How do you know about me?" Nathanael asked.

Jesus replied, "I could see you under the fig tree before Philip found you."

49Then Nathanael exclaimed, "Rabbi, you are the Son of God—the King of Israel!"

50Jesus asked him, "Do you believe this just because I told you I had seen you under the fig tree? You will see greater things than this."

51Then he said, "I tell you the truth, you will all see heaven open and the angels of God going up and down on the Son of Man, the one who is the stairway between heaven and earth."

JESUS: THE MESSIAH

The word *"Messiah"* or *"Christ"* means anointed one. For generations the Jewish people have eagerly waited for the Messiah to come. When He comes, He will make a way for the people to know God in a deep and personal way.

What do we learn about Jesus, "The Word" in verses 1-4 and in verse 14?

_____

_____

_____

_____

What does the title in verse 29 and 36 tell you about Jesus?

_____

_____

_____

_____

What does the title in verse 41 tell you about Jesus?

_____

_____

_____

_____

What did you discover about Jesus today?

_____

_____

_____

_____

_____

DAY TWO

John 2.1-25 (NLT)

Now that you have been introduced to Jesus, John continues with his story. Right off the bat, Jesus began to show that He was no ordinary Rabbi or religious teacher. There was something different about Him. Today you are going to read about two things Jesus did that invoked amazement and anger!

The Wedding at Cana

¹The next day there was a wedding celebration in the village of Cana in Galilee. Jesus' mother was there, ²and Jesus and his disciples were also invited to the celebration. ³The wine supply ran out during the festivities, so Jesus' mother told him, "They have no more wine."

⁴"Dear woman, that's not our problem," Jesus replied. "My time has not yet come."

⁵But his mother told the servants, "Do whatever he tells you."

⁶Standing nearby were six stone water jars, used for Jewish ceremonial washing. Each could hold twenty to thirty gallons.

⁷Jesus told the servants, "Fill the jars with water." When the jars had been filled, ⁸he said, "Now dip some out, and take it to the master of ceremonies." So the servants followed his instructions.

⁹When the master of ceremonies tasted the water that was now wine, not knowing where it had come from (though, of course, the

servants knew), he called the bridegroom over. ¹⁰"A host always serves the best wine first," he said. "Then, when everyone has had a lot to drink, he brings out the less expensive wine. But you have kept the best until now!"
¹¹This miraculous sign at Cana in Galilee was the first time Jesus revealed his glory. And his disciples believed in him.
¹²After the wedding he went to Capernaum for a few days with his mother, his brothers, and his disciples.

Jesus Clears the Temple

¹³It was nearly time for the Jewish Passover celebration, so Jesus went to Jerusalem. ¹⁴In the Temple area he saw merchants selling cattle, sheep, and doves for sacrifices; he also saw dealers at tables exchanging foreign money. ¹⁵Jesus made a whip from some ropes and chased them all out of the Temple. He drove out the sheep and cattle, scattered the money changers' coins over the floor, and turned over their tables.

MONEY CHANGERS:
These people converted regular Jewish currency into a special temple money that was then used to purchase sacrifices to offer in worship. During Jesus' day this changing of money was abused and provided one way to squeeze more money out of honest worshippers who were coming to seek God.

16 Then, going over to the people who sold doves, he told them, "Get these things out of here. Stop turning my Father's house into a marketplace!"
17 Then his disciples remembered this prophecy from the Scriptures: "Passion for God's house will consume me."
18 But the Jewish leaders demanded, "What are you doing? If God gave you authority to do this, show us a miraculous sign to prove it."
19 "All right," Jesus replied. "Destroy this temple, and in three days I will raise it up."
20 "What!" they exclaimed. "It has taken forty-six years to build this Temple, and you can rebuild it in three days?" **21** But when Jesus said "this temple," he meant his own body. **22** After he was raised from the dead, his disciples remembered he had said this, and they believed both the Scriptures and what Jesus had said.

Jesus and Nicodemus
23 Because of the miraculous signs Jesus did in Jerusalem at the Passover celebration, many began to trust in him. **24** But Jesus didn't trust them, because he knew all about people. **25** No one needed to tell him about human nature, for he knew what was in each person's heart.

What does verse 11 say is the reason Jesus performed the miracle?

_____

_____

_____

_____

_____

What was the result of Jesus' miracles according to verse 23?

_____
_____
_____
_____

How did Jesus respond to the group in verse 15?

_____
_____
_____
_____

Why do you think Jesus reacted to them in this way according to verse 16? _____

_____
_____
_____
_____

What did you discover about Jesus today?

_____
_____
_____
_____
_____

DAY THREE

John 3.1-36 (NLT)

Today you are going to see Jesus have a big conversation with a very important man. Nicodemus was a religious leader, a Pharisee (member of the elite and educated ruling class) and a man who had spiritual questions. He decided to explore the claims of Jesus for himself, but he came to Jesus at night so no one would see him. Jesus told Nicodemus some very important things about how to have a relationship with God.

¹There was a man named Nicodemus, a Jewish religious leader who was a Pharisee. ²After dark one evening, he came to speak with Jesus. "Rabbi," he said, "we all know that God has sent you to teach us. Your miraculous signs are evidence that God is with you." ³Jesus replied, "I tell you the truth, unless you are born again, you cannot see the Kingdom of God."
⁴"What do you mean?" exclaimed Nicodemus. "How can an old man go back into his mother's womb and be born again?"
⁵Jesus replied, "I assure you, no one can enter the Kingdom of God without being born of water and the Spirit. ⁶Humans can reproduce only human life, but the Holy Spirit gives birth to spiritual life. ⁷So don't be surprised when I say, 'You must be born again.' ⁸The wind blows wherever it wants. Just as you can hear the wind but can't tell where it comes from or where it is going, so you can't explain how people are born of the Spirit."

BORN AGAIN:
To be *"born again"* means to be made new on the inside, not merely religious on the outside. Just as you were born physically when you came into this world, you must also be born spiritually into God's family by faith in Jesus.

⁹How are these things possible?" Nicodemus asked. ¹⁰Jesus replied, "You are a respected Jewish teacher, and yet you don't understand these things? ¹¹I assure you, we tell you what we know and have seen, and yet you won't believe our testimony. ¹² But if you don't believe me when I tell you about earthly things, how can you possibly believe if I tell you about heavenly things? ¹³No one has ever gone to heaven and returned. But the Son of Man has come down from heaven. ¹⁴And as Moses lifted up the bronze snake on a pole in the wilderness, so the Son of Man must be lifted up, ¹⁵so that everyone who believes in him will have eternal life.

JESUS: SON OF MAN
This is another title of Jesus. It refers to the Messiah, the one who was to come from God.

¹⁶"For this is how God loved the world: He gave his one and only Son, so that everyone who believes in him will not perish but have

eternal life. **17**God sent his Son into the world not to judge the world, but to save the world through him.

18"There is no judgment against anyone who believes in him. But anyone who does not believe in him has already been judged for not believing in God's one and only Son. **19**And the judgment is based on this fact: God's light came into the world, but people loved the darkness more than the light, for their actions were evil. **20**All who do evil hate the light and refuse to go near it for fear their sins will be exposed. **21**But those who do what is right come to the light so others can see that they are doing what God wants."

John the Baptist Exalts Jesus

22Then Jesus and his disciples left Jerusalem and went into the Judean countryside. Jesus spent some time with them there, baptizing people.

23At this time John the Baptist was baptizing at Aenon, near Salim, because there was plenty of water there; and people kept coming to him for baptism. **24**(This was before John was thrown into prison.) **25**A debate broke out between John's disciples and a certain Jew over ceremonial cleansing. **26**So John's disciples came to him and said, "Rabbi, the man you met on the other side of the Jordan River, the one you identified as the Messiah, is also baptizing people. And everybody is going to him instead of coming to us."

27John replied, "No one can receive anything unless God gives it from heaven. **28**You yourselves know how plainly I told you, 'I am not the Messiah. I am only here to prepare the way for him.' **29**It is the bridegroom who marries the bride, and the bridegroom's friend is simply glad to stand with him and hear his vows. Therefore, I am filled with joy at his success. **30**He must become greater and greater, and I must become less and less.

³¹"He has come from above and is greater than anyone else. We are of the earth, and we speak of earthly things, but he has come from heaven and is greater than anyone else. ³²He testifies about what he has seen and heard, but how few believe what he tells them! ³³Anyone who accepts his testimony can affirm that God is true. ³⁴For he is sent by God. He speaks God's words, for God gives him the Spirit without limit. ³⁵The Father loves his Son and has put everything into his hands. ³⁶And anyone who believes in God's Son has eternal life. Anyone who doesn't obey the Son will never experience eternal life but remains under God's angry judgment."

What do you learn about Jesus in verse 13?

_____
_____
_____
_____
_____
_____
_____

John 3.16-19: These are some of the most familiar verses in the Bible. **What do these verses say about why God sent Jesus into the world?**

_____
_____
_____

What do these verses tell you about how to have eternal life?

What do they say about people who reject Jesus?

DAY FOUR

John 4.1-54 (NLT)

Yesterday Jesus had a very important conversation with a powerful, wealthy and educated man. Today Jesus is going to have another conversation, but this time with an insignificant, marginalized and poor woman. What He tells this woman will completely change her and her community.

Jesus and the Samaritan Woman

¹Jesus knew the Pharisees had heard that he was baptizing and making more disciples than John ²(though Jesus himself didn't baptize them—his disciples did). ³So he left Judea and returned to Galilee.
⁴He had to go through Samaria on the way. ⁵Eventually he came to the Samaritan village of Sychar, near the field that Jacob gave to his son Joseph. ⁶Jacob's well was there; and Jesus, tired from the long walk, sat wearily beside the well about noontime. ⁷Soon a Samaritan woman came to draw water, and Jesus said to her, "Please give me a drink." ⁸He was alone at the time because his disciples had gone into the village to buy some food.
⁹The woman was surprised, for Jews refuse to have anything to do with Samaritans.

SAMARITANS:
This was a group who were a mix of Jewish and non-Jewish people, and broke off from Israel to set up their own system of worship. Because of this, they were greatly looked down on by the Jewish people.

She said to Jesus, "You are a Jew, and I am a Samaritan woman. Why are you asking me for a drink?"
¹⁰Jesus replied, "If you only knew the gift God has for you and who you are speaking to, you would ask me, and I would give you living water."
¹¹"But sir, you don't have a rope or a bucket," she said, "and this well is very deep. Where would you get this living water? ¹²And besides, do you think you're greater than our ancestor Jacob, who gave us this well? How can you offer better water than he and his sons and his animals enjoyed?"
¹³ Jesus replied, "Anyone who drinks this water will soon become thirsty again. ¹⁴But those who drink the water I give will never be thirsty again. It becomes a fresh, bubbling spring within them, giving them eternal life."
¹⁵"Please, sir," the woman said, "give me this water! Then I'll never be thirsty again, and I won't have to come here to get water."
¹⁶"Go and get your husband," Jesus told her.
¹⁷"I don't have a husband," the woman replied.
Jesus said, "You're right! You don't have a husband— ¹⁸for you have had five husbands, and you aren't even married to the man you're living with now. You certainly spoke the truth!"
¹⁹"Sir," the woman said, "you must be a prophet. ²⁰So tell me, why

is it that you Jews insist that Jerusalem is the only place of worship, while we Samaritans claim it is here at Mount Gerizim, where our ancestors worshiped?"
21 Jesus replied, "Believe me, dear woman, the time is coming when it will no longer matter whether you worship the Father on this mountain or in Jerusalem. **22**You Samaritans know very little about the one you worship, while we Jews know all about him, for salvation comes through the Jews. **23**But the time is coming—indeed it's here now—when true worshipers will worship the Father in spirit and in truth. The Father is looking for those who will worship him that way. **24**For God is Spirit, so those who worship him must worship in spirit and in truth."
25The woman said, "I know the Messiah is coming—the one who is called Christ. When he comes, he will explain everything to us."
26Then Jesus told her, "I am the Messiah!"
27Just then his disciples came back. They were shocked to find him talking to a woman, but none of them had the nerve to ask, "What do you want with her?" or "Why are you talking to her?"
28The woman left her water jar beside the well and ran back to the village, telling everyone, **29**"Come and see a man who told me everything I ever did! Could he possibly be the Messiah?" **30**So the people came streaming from the village to see him.
31Meanwhile, the disciples were urging Jesus, "Rabbi, eat something."
32But Jesus replied, "I have a kind of food you know nothing about."
33"Did someone bring him food while we were gone?" the disciples asked each other.
34Then Jesus explained: "My nourishment comes from doing the will of God, who sent me, and from finishing his work. **35**You know the saying, 'Four months between planting and harvest.' But I say,

wake up and look around. The fields are already ripe for harvest. **36**The harvesters are paid good wages, and the fruit they harvest is people brought to eternal life. What joy awaits both the planter and the harvester alike! **37**You know the saying, 'One plants and another harvests.' And it's true. **38**I sent you to harvest where you didn't plant; others had already done the work, and now you will get to gather the harvest."

Many Samaritans Believe

39Many Samaritans from the village believed in Jesus because the woman had said, "He told me everything I ever did!" **40**When they came out to see him, they begged him to stay in their village. So he stayed for two days, **41**long enough for many more to hear his message and believe. **42**Then they said to the woman, "Now we believe, not just because of what you told us, but because we have heard him ourselves. Now we know that he is indeed the Savior of the world."

Jesus Heals an Official's Son

43At the end of the two days, Jesus went on to Galilee. **44**He himself had said that a prophet is not honored in his own hometown. **45**Yet the Galileans welcomed him, for they had been in Jerusalem at the Passover celebration and had seen everything he did there. **46**As he traveled through Galilee, he came to Cana, where he had turned the water into wine. There was a government official in nearby Capernaum whose son was very sick. **47**When he heard that Jesus had come from Judea to Galilee, he went and begged Jesus to come to Capernaum to heal his son, who was about to die. **48**Jesus asked, "Will you never believe in me unless you see miraculous signs and wonders?"

⁴⁹The official pleaded, "Lord, please come now before my little boy dies."
⁵⁰Then Jesus told him, "Go back home. Your son will live!" And the man believed what Jesus said and started home.
⁵¹While the man was on his way, some of his servants met him with the news that his son was alive and well. **⁵²**He asked them when the boy had begun to get better, and they replied, "Yesterday afternoon at one o'clock his fever suddenly disappeared!" **⁵³**Then the father realized that that was the very time Jesus had told him, "Your son will live." And he and his entire household believed in Jesus. **⁵⁴**This was the second miraculous sign Jesus did in Galilee after coming from Judea.

What do you think Jesus was offering this woman in verse 10?

_____
_____
_____
_____
_____

Why do you think Jesus exposed this woman's hidden past in verses 16-18? _____

_____
_____
_____
_____

What did Jesus reveal to this woman in verse 26?

_____
_____
_____
_____
_____
_____
_____
_____
_____

How did the people respond to Jesus in verses 39-42?

_____
_____
_____
_____
_____
_____
_____
_____
_____
_____
_____
_____

DAY FIVE

John 5.1-47 (NLT)

Jesus wasn't afraid to reveal His true identity, even when it brought out a negative reaction. Today you are going to see how Jesus engages in a bold discussion with the religious leaders of His day. Jesus makes some bold, audacious and shocking statements. One thing is for sure, Jesus didn't leave any middle ground. You either believe Him or you don't.

Jesus Heals a Lame Man
¹Afterward Jesus returned to Jerusalem for one of the Jewish holy days. ²Inside the city, near the Sheep Gate, was the pool of Bethesda, with five covered porches. ³Crowds of sick people—blind, lame, or paralyzed—lay on the porches. ⁵One of the men lying there had been sick for thirty-eight years. ⁶When Jesus saw him and knew he had been ill for a long time, he asked him, "Would you like to get well?"
⁷"I can't, sir," the sick man said, "for I have no one to put me into the pool when the water bubbles up. Someone else always gets there ahead of me."
⁸Jesus told him, "Stand up, pick up your mat, and walk!"
⁹Instantly, the man was healed! He rolled up his sleeping mat and began walking! But this miracle happened on the Sabbath, ¹⁰so the Jewish leaders objected. They said to the man who was cured,

"You can't work on the Sabbath! The law doesn't allow you to carry that sleeping mat!"

¹¹But he replied, "The man who healed me told me, 'Pick up your mat and walk.'"

¹²"Who said such a thing as that?" they demanded.

¹³The man didn't know, for Jesus had disappeared into the crowd. ¹⁴But afterward Jesus found him in the Temple and told him, "Now you are well; so stop sinning, or something even worse may happen to you." ¹⁵Then the man went and told the Jewish leaders that it was Jesus who had healed him.

Jesus Claims to Be the Son of God

¹⁶So the Jewish leaders began harassing Jesus for breaking the Sabbath rules. ¹⁷But Jesus replied, "My Father is always working, and so am I." ¹⁸So the Jewish leaders tried all the harder to find a way to kill him. For he not only broke the Sabbath, he called God his Father, thereby making himself equal with God. ¹⁹So Jesus explained, "I tell you the truth, the Son can do nothing by himself. He does only what he sees the Father doing. Whatever the Father does, the Son also does.

SABBATH RULES:
The Sabbath was the traditional day of rest for the Jewish people. No one could work on this day. When Jesus healed on the Sabbath, the religious leaders were more concerned about Jesus breaking their rules than the fact that He was helping a person.

²⁰For the Father loves the Son and shows him everything he is doing. In fact, the Father will show him how to do even greater works than healing this man. Then you will truly be astonished.

²¹For just as the Father gives life to those he raises from the dead, so the Son gives life to anyone he wants. ²²In addition, the Father

JESUS: THE SON OF GOD

Jesus claimed to be the Son of God who came down from His Father in Heaven.

judges no one. Instead, he has given the Son absolute authority to judge, **23**so that everyone will honor the Son, just as they honor the Father. Anyone who does not honor the Son is certainly not honoring the Father who sent him.
24"I tell you the truth, those who listen to my message and believe in God who sent me have eternal life. They will never be condemned for their sins, but they have already passed from death into life.
25"And I assure you that the time is coming, indeed it's here now, when the dead will hear my voice—the voice of the Son of God. And those who listen will live. **26**The Father has life in himself, and he has granted that same life-giving power to his Son. **27**And he has given him authority to judge everyone because he is the Son of Man. **28**Don't be so surprised! Indeed, the time is coming when all the dead in their graves will hear the voice of God's Son, **29**and they will rise again. Those who have done good will rise to experience eternal life, and those who have continued in evil will rise to experience judgment. **30**I can do nothing on my own. I judge as God tells me. Therefore, my judgment is just, because I carry out the will of the one who sent me, not my own will.

Witnesses to Jesus

31 "If I were to testify on my own behalf, my testimony would not be valid. **32** But someone else is also testifying about me, and I assure you that everything he says about me is true. **33** In fact, you sent investigators to listen to John the Baptist, and his testimony about me was true. **34** Of course, I have no need of human witnesses, but I say these things so you might be saved. **35** John was like a burning and shining lamp, and you were excited for a while about his message. **36** But I have a greater witness than John—my teachings and my miracles. The Father gave me these works to accomplish, and they prove that he sent me. **37** And the Father who sent me has testified about me himself. You have never heard his voice or seen him face to face, **38** and you do not have his message in your hearts, because you do not believe me—the one he sent to you.

39 "You search the Scriptures because you think they give you eternal life. But the Scriptures point to me! **40** Yet you refuse to come to me to receive this life.

41 "Your approval means nothing to me, **42** because I know you don't have God's love within you. **43** For I have come to you in my Father's name, and you have rejected me. Yet if others come in their own name, you gladly welcome them. **44** No wonder you can't believe! For you gladly honor each other, but you don't care about the honor that comes from the one who alone is God.

45 "Yet it isn't I who will accuse you before the Father. Moses will accuse you! Yes, Moses, in whom you put your hopes. **46** If you really believed Moses, you would believe me, because he wrote about me. **47** But since you don't believe what he wrote, how will you believe what I say?"

What do you learn about Jesus as the Son of God in verses 19-23?

_____

_____

_____

_____

What must a person do to have eternal life according to verse 24?

_____

_____

_____

_____

What is the purpose of the scriptures (the Bible) according to verses 39-40? _____

_____

_____

_____

_____

How do you feel about these bold claims of Jesus?

_____

_____

_____

_____

_____

DAY SIX

John 6.1-71 (NLT)

Jesus did many miraculous things. Today you are going to see two major miracles of Jesus – feeding of 5000 people and walking on the water. Hint: Every miracle of Jesus reveals something about who He is and what He wants to do in your life. Also, you are about to come across some of the hard sayings of Jesus. As you read, ask God to help you understand what Jesus is saying.

Jesus Feeds Five Thousand

¹After this, Jesus crossed over to the far side of the Sea of Galilee, also known as the Sea of Tiberias.
²A huge crowd kept following him wherever he went, because they saw his miraculous signs as he healed the sick.
³Then Jesus climbed a hill and sat down with his disciples around him. ⁴(It was nearly time for the Jewish Passover celebration.) ⁵Jesus soon saw a huge crowd of people coming to look for him. Turning to Philip, he asked, "Where can we buy bread to feed all these people?" ⁶He was testing Philip, for he already knew what he was going to do. ⁷Philip replied, "Even if we worked for months, we wouldn't have enough money to feed them!"

THE SEA OF GALILEE:
Also called the Sea of Tiberias or Lake Genessaret, it is a large lake located on the northern end of Israel. Still today, rolling mountains, grassy slopes and palm trees surround it.

8Then Andrew, Simon Peter's brother, spoke up. **9**"There's a young boy here with five barley loaves and two fish. But what good is that with this huge crowd?"
10"Tell everyone to sit down," Jesus said. So they all sat down on the grassy slopes. (The men alone numbered about 5,000.) **11**Then Jesus took the loaves, gave thanks to God, and distributed them to the people. Afterward he did the same with the fish. And they all ate as much as they wanted. **12**After everyone was full, Jesus told his disciples, "Now gather the leftovers, so that nothing is wasted." **13**So they picked up the pieces and filled twelve baskets with scraps left by the people who had eaten from the five barley loaves.
14When the people saw him do this miraculous sign, they exclaimed, "Surely, he is the Prophet we have been expecting!" **15**When Jesus saw that they were ready to force him to be their king, he slipped away into the hills by himself.

Jesus Walks on Water

16That evening Jesus' disciples went down to the shore to wait for him. **17**But as darkness fell and Jesus still hadn't come back, they got into the boat and headed across the lake toward Capernaum. **18**Soon a gale swept down upon them, and the sea grew very rough. **19**They had rowed three or four miles when suddenly they saw Jesus walking on the water toward the boat. They were terrified, **20**but he called out to them, "Don't be afraid. I am here!" **21**Then they were eager to let him in the boat, and immediately they arrived at their destination!

Jesus, the Bread of Life

22The next day the crowd that had stayed on the far shore saw that the disciples had taken the only boat, and they realized Jesus had not gone with them. **23**Several boats from Tiberias landed near the place where the Lord had blessed the bread and the people had eaten.

24So when the crowd saw that neither Jesus nor his disciples were there, they got into the boats and went across to Capernaum to look for him. **25**They found him on the other side of the lake and asked, "Rabbi, when did you get here?"

26Jesus replied, "I tell you the truth, you want to be with me because I fed you, not because you understood the miraculous signs. **27**But don't be so concerned about perishable things like food. Spend your energy seeking the eternal life that the Son of Man can give you. For God the Father has given me the seal of his approval."

28They replied, "We want to perform God's works, too. What should we do?"

29Jesus told them, "This is the only work God wants from you: Believe in the one he has sent."

30They answered, "Show us a miraculous sign if you want us to believe in you. What can you do? **31**After all, our ancestors ate manna while they journeyed through the wilderness! The Scriptures say, 'Moses gave them bread from heaven to eat.'"

MANNA:

God provided Manna to feed the Israelites as they wandered in the wilderness for 40 years. Manna was a bread-like substance that settled on the desert floor at night. It was *"bread from Heaven."*

32Jesus said, "I tell you the truth, Moses didn't give you bread from heaven. My Father did. And now he offers you the true bread from heaven. **33**The true bread of God is the one who comes down from heaven and gives life to the world."

34"Sir," they said, "give us that bread every day."
35Jesus replied, "I am the bread of life. Whoever comes to me will never be hungry again. Whoever believes in me will never be thirsty. **36**But you haven't believed in me even though you have seen me. **37**However, those the Father has given me will come to me, and I will never reject them. **38**For I have come down from heaven to do the will of God who sent me, not to do my own will. **39**And this is the will of God, that I should not lose even one of all those he has given me, but that I should raise them up at the last day. **40**For it is my Father's will that all who see his Son and believe in him should have eternal life. I will raise them up at the last day."
41Then the people began to murmur in disagreement because he had said, "I am the bread that came down from heaven." **42**They said, "Isn't this Jesus, the son of Joseph? We know his father and mother. How can he say, 'I came down from heaven'?"
43But Jesus replied, "Stop complaining about what I said. **44**For no one can come to me unless the Father who sent me draws them to me, and at the last day I will raise them up. **45**As it is written in the Scriptures, 'They will all be taught by God.' Everyone who listens to the Father and learns from him comes to me. **46**(Not that anyone has ever seen the Father; only I, who was sent from God, have seen him.) **47**"I tell you the truth, anyone who believes has eternal life. **48**Yes, I am the bread of life! **49**Your ancestors ate manna in the wilderness, but they all died. **50**Anyone who eats the bread from heaven, however, will never die. **51**I am the living bread that came down from heaven. Anyone who eats this bread will live forever; and this bread, which I will offer so the world may live, is my flesh."
52Then the people began arguing with each other about what he meant. "How can this man give us his flesh to eat?" they asked.
53So Jesus said again, "I tell you the truth, unless you eat the flesh of the Son of Man and drink his blood, you cannot have eternal life

within you. **⁵⁴**But anyone who eats my flesh and drinks my blood has eternal life, and I will raise that person at the last day. **⁵⁵**For my flesh is true food, and my blood is true drink. **⁵⁶**Anyone who eats my flesh and drinks my blood remains in me, and I in him.

EAT MY FLESH:
Jesus is speaking symbolically here. Just as the Israelites ate (or received) the manna from Heaven and were saved from dying in the desert, so those who receive Jesus and believe in Him are saved from their sin and find eternal life.

⁵⁷I live because of the living Father who sent me; in the same way, anyone who feeds on me will live because of me. **⁵⁸**I am the true bread that came down from heaven. Anyone who eats this bread will not die as your ancestors did (even though they ate the manna) but will live forever." **⁵⁹**He said these things while he was teaching in the synagogue in Capernaum.

Many Disciples Desert Jesus
⁶⁰Many of his disciples said, "This is very hard to understand. How can anyone accept it?"

⁶¹ Jesus was aware that his disciples were complaining, so he said to them, "Does this offend you? **⁶²**Then what will you think if you see the Son of Man ascend to heaven again? **⁶³**The Spirit alone gives eternal life. Human effort accomplishes nothing. And the very words I have spoken to you are spirit and life. **⁶⁴**But some of you do not believe me." (For Jesus knew from the beginning which ones didn't believe, and he knew who would betray him.) **⁶⁵** Then he said, "That is why I said that people can't come to me unless the Father gives them to me."

⁶⁶At this point many of his disciples turned away and deserted him.

⁶⁷ Then Jesus turned to the Twelve and asked, "Are you also going to leave?" ⁶⁸Simon Peter replied, "Lord, to whom would we go? You have the words that give eternal life. ⁶⁹We believe, and we know you are the Holy One of God."

⁷⁰Then Jesus said, "I chose the twelve of you, but one is a devil." ⁷¹He was speaking of Judas, son of Simon Iscariot, one of the Twelve, who would later betray him.

What did Jesus do with what the young boy put in His hands according to verse 11? Just think what Jesus could do if you put your life in His hands!

_____

_____

_____

Why do you think Jesus came to them walking on the water (see verses 18-20)?

_____

_____

_____

What was wrong with the way these people approached Jesus in verses 26-27? Do people still come to Jesus in the same way today?

_____

_____

_____

_____

What does God want from you according to verse 29?

What does Jesus reveal about Himself in verses 47-51?

How did people respond to Jesus' hard sayings in verses 66-69?

DAY SEVEN

John 7.1-53 (NLT)

In this passage, Jesus travels to Jerusalem to participate in the Jewish Festival of the Tabernacles (or Shelters). This was one of the major festivals in the Jewish year. As He enters Jerusalem, people are divided over Jesus. Some think He is crazy, others believe that He is truly the Son of God and the promised Messiah. Still today people are divided over Jesus. As you read, reflect on what you believe to be true about Jesus.

Jesus and His Brothers

1After this, Jesus traveled around Galilee. He wanted to stay out of Judea, where the Jewish leaders were plotting his death. **2**But soon it was time for the Jewish Festival of Shelters, **3**and Jesus' brothers said to him, "Leave here and go to Judea, where your followers can see your miracles! **4**You can't become famous if you hide like this! If you can do such wonderful things, show yourself to the world!" **5**For even his brothers didn't believe in him.

6Jesus replied, "Now is not the right time for me to go, but you can go anytime. **7**The world can't hate you, but it does hate me because I accuse it of doing evil. **8**You go on. I'm not going to this festival, because my time has not yet come." **9**After saying these things, Jesus remained in Galilee.

Jesus Teaches Openly at the Temple

10But after his brothers left for the festival, Jesus also went, though secretly, staying out of public view. **11**The Jewish leaders tried to find him at the festival and kept asking if anyone had seen him. **12**There was a lot of grumbling about him among the crowds. Some argued, "He's a good man," but others said, "He's nothing but a fraud who deceives the people." **13**But no one had the courage to speak favorably about him in public, for they were afraid of getting in trouble with the Jewish leaders.

14Then, midway through the festival, Jesus went up to the Temple and began to teach. **15**The people were surprised when they heard him. "How does he know so much when he hasn't been trained?" they asked.

16So Jesus told them, "My message is not my own; it comes from God who sent me. **17**Anyone who wants to do the will of God will know whether my teaching is from God or is merely my own. **18**Those who speak for themselves want glory only for themselves, but a person who seeks to honor the one who sent him speaks truth, not lies. **19**Moses gave you the law, but none of you obeys it! In fact, you are trying to kill me."

20The crowd replied, "You're demon possessed! Who's trying to kill you?"

21Jesus replied, "I did one miracle on the Sabbath, and you were amazed. **22**But you work on the Sabbath, too, when you obey Moses' law of circumcision. (Actually, this tradition of circumcision began with the patriarchs, long before the law of Moses.) **23**For if the correct time for circumcising your son falls on the Sabbath, you go ahead and do it so as not to break the law of Moses. So why should you be angry with me for healing a man on the Sabbath? **24**Look beneath the surface so you can judge correctly."

Is Jesus the Messiah?

²⁵Some of the people who lived in Jerusalem started to ask each other, "Isn't this the man they are trying to kill? ²⁶But here he is, speaking in public, and they say nothing to him. Could our leaders possibly believe that he is the Messiah? ²⁷But how could he be? For we know where this man comes from. When the Messiah comes, he will simply appear; no one will know where he comes from."
²⁸While Jesus was teaching in the Temple, he called out, "Yes, you know me, and you know where I come from. But I'm not here on my own. The one who sent me is true, and you don't know him. ²⁹But I know him because I come from him, and he sent me to you."
³⁰Then the leaders tried to arrest him; but no one laid a hand on him, because his time had not yet come.
³¹Many among the crowds at the Temple believed in him. "After all," they said, "would you expect the Messiah to do more miraculous signs than this man has done?"
³²When the Pharisees heard that the crowds were whispering such things, they and the leading priests sent Temple guards to arrest Jesus. ³³But Jesus told them, "I will be with you only a little longer. Then I will return to the one who sent me. ³⁴You will search for me but not find me. And you cannot go where I am going."
³⁵The Jewish leaders were puzzled by this statement. "Where is he planning to go?" they asked. "Is he thinking of leaving the country and going to the Jews in other lands? Maybe he will even teach the Greeks! ³⁶What does he mean when he says, 'You will search for me but not find me,' and 'You cannot go where I am going'?"

Jesus Promises Living Water

³⁷On the last day, the climax of the festival, Jesus stood and shouted to the crowds, "Anyone who is thirsty may come to me! ³⁸Anyone who believes in me may come and drink! For the Scriptures declare,

'Rivers of living water will flow from his heart.'" **39**(When he said "living water," he was speaking of the Spirit, who would be given to everyone believing in him. But the Spirit had not yet been given, because Jesus had not yet entered into his glory.)

Division and Unbelief

40When the crowds heard him say this, some of them declared, "Surely this man is the Prophet we've been expecting." **41**Others said, "He is the Messiah." Still others said, "But he can't be! Will the Messiah come from Galilee? **42**For the Scriptures clearly state that the Messiah will be born of the royal line of David, in Bethlehem, the village where King David was born." **43**So the crowd was divided about him. **44**Some even wanted him arrested, but no one laid a hand on him.

45When the Temple guards returned without having arrested Jesus, the leading priests and Pharisees demanded, "Why didn't you bring him in?"

46"We have never heard anyone speak like this!" the guards responded.

47"Have you been led astray, too?" the Pharisees mocked. **48**"Is there a single one of us rulers or Pharisees who believes in him? **49**This foolish crowd follows him, but they are ignorant of the law. God's curse is on them!"

50Then Nicodemus, the leader who had met with Jesus earlier, spoke up. **51**"Is it legal to convict a man before he is given a hearing?" he asked.

52They replied, "Are you from Galilee, too? Search the Scriptures and see for yourself—no prophet ever comes from Galilee!"

[The most ancient Greek manuscripts do not include John 7:53–8:11.]
53Then the meeting broke up, and everybody went home.

What did Jesus mean when He said, "…my time has not yet come?" in verse 8? _____

_____

_____

What invitation did Jesus give to the people in verse 38?

_____

_____

_____

What were some of the different views of Jesus in His day?

_____

_____

_____

What do you think about Jesus so far? _____

_____

_____

_____

_____

_____

_____

_____

_____

DAY EIGHT

John 8.1-59 (NLT)

Jesus was compassionate and courageous. To those who humbly trusted Him, Jesus showed tremendous compassion and grace, but to those who stubbornly rejected Him, Jesus responded with harsh warnings. Today you are going to see both sides of Jesus. You will see Him tender to a broken woman, and hard toward unbelieving and resistant leaders. Think about how you should approach Jesus today.

A Woman Caught in Adultery

¹Jesus returned to the Mount of Olives, ²but early the next morning he was back again at the Temple. A crowd soon gathered, and he sat down and taught them. ³As he was speaking, the teachers of religious law and the Pharisees brought a woman who had been caught in the act of adultery. They put her in front of the crowd. ⁴"Teacher," they said to Jesus, "this woman was caught in the act of adultery. ⁵The law of Moses says to stone her. What do you say?" ⁶They were trying to trap him into saying something they could use against him, but Jesus stooped down and wrote in the dust with his finger. ⁷They kept demanding an answer, so he stood up again and said, "All right, but let the one who has never sinned throw the first stone!" ⁸Then he stooped down again and wrote in the dust. ⁹When the accusers heard this, they slipped away one by one, beginning with the oldest, until only Jesus was left in the middle of

the crowd with the woman. **10**Then Jesus stood up again and said to the woman, "Where are your accusers? Didn't even one of them condemn you?"
11"No, Lord," she said.
And Jesus said, "Neither do I. Go and sin no more."

Jesus, the Light of the World
12Jesus spoke to the people once more and said, "I am the light of the world. If you follow me, you won't have to walk in darkness, because you will have the light that leads to life."
13The Pharisees replied, "You are making those claims about yourself! Such testimony is not valid."
14Jesus told them, "These claims are valid even though I make them about myself. For I know where I came from and where I am going, but you don't know this about me. **15**You judge me by human standards, but I do not judge anyone. **16**And if I did, my judgment would be correct in every respect because I am not alone. The Father who sent me is with me. **17**Your own law says that if two people agree about something, their witness is accepted as fact. **18**I am one witness, and my Father who sent me is the other."
19"Where is your father?" they asked.
Jesus answered, "Since you don't know who I am, you don't know who my Father is. If you knew me, you would also know my Father."
20Jesus made these statements while he was teaching in the section of the Temple known as the Treasury. But he was not arrested, because his time had not yet come.

The Unbelieving People Warned
21Later Jesus said to them again, "I am going away. You will search for me but will die in your sin. You cannot come where I am going."
22The people asked, "Is he planning to commit suicide? What does

he mean, 'You cannot come where I am going'?"
²³Jesus continued, "You are from below; I am from above. You belong to this world; I do not. ²⁴That is why I said that you will die in your sins; for unless you believe that I am who I claim to be, you will die in your sins."
²⁵"Who are you?" they demanded.
Jesus replied, "The one I have always claimed to be. ²⁶I have much to say about you and much to condemn, but I won't. For I say only what I have heard from the one who sent me, and he is completely truthful." ²⁷But they still didn't understand that he was talking about his Father.
²⁸So Jesus said, "When you have lifted up the Son of Man on the cross, then you will understand that I am he. I do nothing on my own but say only what the Father taught me. ²⁹And the one who sent me is with me—he has not deserted me. For I always do what pleases him." ³⁰Then many who heard him say these things believed in him.

Jesus and Abraham

³¹Jesus said to the people who believed in him, "You are truly my disciples if you remain faithful to my teachings. ³²And you will know the truth, and the truth will set you free."
³³"But we are descendants of Abraham," they said. "We have never been slaves to anyone. What do you mean, 'You will be set free'?"
³⁴Jesus replied, "I tell you the truth, everyone who sins is a slave of sin. ³⁵A slave is not a permanent member of the family, but a son is part of the family forever.
³⁶So if the Son sets you free, you are truly free.

SIN:
Sin was an archery term that meant to miss the bullseye. Later, it became the term used for the things that we do that are wrong and separate us from God.

37Yes, I realize that you are descendants of Abraham. And yet some of you are trying to kill me because there's no room in your hearts for my message. **38**I am telling you what I saw when I was with my Father. But you are following the advice of your father."
39"Our father is Abraham!" they declared.

"No," Jesus replied, "for if you were really the children of Abraham, you would follow his example. **40**Instead, you are trying to kill me because I told you the truth, which I heard from God. Abraham never did such a thing. **41**No, you are imitating your real father." They replied, "We aren't illegitimate children! God himself is our true Father."

42Jesus told them, "If God were your Father, you would love me, because I have come to you from God. I am not here on my own, but he sent me. **43**Why can't you understand what I am saying? It's because you can't even hear me! **44**For you are the children of your father the devil, and you love to do the evil things he does. He was a murderer from the beginning. He has always hated the truth, because there is no truth in him. When he lies, it is consistent with his character; for he is a liar and the father of lies. **45**So when I tell the truth, you just naturally don't believe me! **46**Which of you can truthfully accuse me of sin? And since I am telling you the truth, why don't you believe me? **47**Anyone who belongs to God listens gladly to the words of God. But you don't listen because you don't belong to God."

48The people retorted, "You Samaritan devil! Didn't we say all along that you were possessed by a demon?"

49"No," Jesus said, "I have no demon in me. For I honor my Father—and you dishonor me. **50**And though I have no wish to glorify myself, God is going to glorify me. He is the true judge. **51**I tell you the truth, anyone who obeys my teaching will never die!"

52The people said, "Now we know you are possessed by a

demon. Even Abraham and the prophets died, but you say, 'Anyone who obeys my teaching will never die!' ⁵³Are you greater than our father Abraham? He died, and so did the prophets. Who do you think you are?"

⁵⁴ Jesus answered, "If I want glory for myself, it doesn't count. But it is my Father who will glorify me. You say, 'He is our God,' ⁵⁵but you don't even know him. I know him. If I said otherwise, I would be as great a liar as you! But I do know him and obey him. ⁵⁶Your father Abraham rejoiced as he looked forward to my coming. He saw it and was glad."

⁵⁷ The people said, "You aren't even fifty years old. How can you say you have seen Abraham?"

⁵⁸ Jesus answered, "I tell you the truth, before Abraham was even born, I am!" ⁵⁹At that point they picked up stones to throw at him. But Jesus was hidden from them and left the Temple.

What does the encounter in verses 1-11 tell you about how Jesus feels about you when you fail? _____

_____

_____

_____

What did Jesus reveal about Himself in verse 23?

_____

_____

_____

What is the warning Jesus gives in verse 24?

_____
_____
_____
_____

What did Jesus say about sin in verses 35-36?

_____
_____
_____

What bold claim did Jesus make about Himself in verses 56-58?

_____
_____
_____

What was the people's response to Jesus in verse 59?

_____
_____
_____

What do you think about this claim of Jesus?

_____
_____
_____
_____

DAY NINE

John 9.1-41 (NLT)

Have you ever tried to walk around in a room that is pitch black? It's easy to stumble over things and run into walls, because you simply can't see. In the same way, there are people who are in the dark spiritually and can't see who Jesus is. In this reading, you are going to meet a man who was born blind but found spiritual sight; and a group of people who were born with physical sight but were spiritually blind. Ask God to open your eyes to see the truth about Jesus.

Jesus Heals a Man Born Blind

¹As Jesus was walking along, he saw a man who had been blind from birth. ²"Rabbi," his disciples asked him, "why was this man born blind? Was it because of his own sins or his parents' sins?" ³"It was not because of his sins or his parents' sins," Jesus answered. "This happened so the power of God could be seen in him. ⁴We must quickly carry out the tasks assigned us by the one who sent us. The night is coming, and then no one can work. ⁵But while I am here in the world, I am the light of the world."

⁶Then he spit on the ground, made mud with the saliva, and spread the mud over the blind man's eyes. ⁷He told him, "Go wash yourself in the pool of Siloam" (Siloam means "sent"). So the man went and washed and came back seeing!

8His neighbors and others who knew him as a blind beggar asked each other, "Isn't this the man who used to sit and beg?" **9**Some said he was, and others said, "No, he just looks like him!"

But the beggar kept saying, "Yes, I am the same one!"

10They asked, "Who healed you? What happened?"

11He told them, "The man they call Jesus made mud and spread it over my eyes and told me, 'Go to the pool of Siloam and wash yourself.' So I went and washed, and now I can see!"

12"Where is he now?" they asked.

"I don't know," he replied.

13Then they took the man who had been blind to the Pharisees, **14**because it was on the Sabbath that Jesus had made the mud and healed him. **15**The Pharisees asked the man all about it. So he told them, "He put the mud over my eyes, and when I washed it away, I could see!"

16Some of the Pharisees said, "This man Jesus is not from God, for he is working on the Sabbath." Others said, "But how could an ordinary sinner do such miraculous signs?" So there was a deep division of opinion among them

17Then the Pharisees again questioned the man who had been blind and demanded, "What's your opinion about this man who healed you?"

The man replied, "I think he must be a prophet."

18The Jewish leaders still refused to believe the man had been blind and could now see, so they called in his parents.

19They asked them, "Is this your son? Was he born blind? If so, how can he now see?"

20His parents replied, "We know this is our son and that he was born blind, **21**but we don't know how he can see or who healed him. Ask him. He is old enough to speak for himself." **22**His parents said this because they were afraid of the Jewish leaders, who had announced that anyone saying Jesus was the Messiah would be expelled from the synagogue. ²³That's why they said, "He is old enough. Ask him."

²⁴So for the second time they called in the man who had been blind and told him, "God should get the glory for this, because we know this man Jesus is a sinner."

²⁵"I don't know whether he is a sinner," the man replied. "But I know this: I was blind, and now I can see!"

²⁶"But what did he do?" they asked. "How did he heal you?"

²⁷"Look!" the man exclaimed. "I told you once. Didn't you listen? Why do you want to hear it again? Do you want to become his disciples, too?"

²⁸Then they cursed him and said, "You are his disciple, but we are disciples of Moses! ²⁹We know God spoke to Moses, but we don't even know where this man comes from."

³⁰"Why, that's very strange!" the man replied. "He healed my eyes, and yet you don't know where he comes from? ³¹We know that God doesn't listen to sinners, but he is ready to hear those who worship him and do his will. ³²Ever since the world began, no one has been able to open the eyes of someone born blind. ³³If this man were not from God, he couldn't have done it."

³⁴"You were born a total sinner!" they answered. "Are you trying to teach us?" And they threw him out of the synagogue.

Spiritual Blindness

³⁵When Jesus heard what had happened, he found the man and asked, "Do you believe in the Son of Man?"

³⁶The man answered, "Who is he, sir? I want to believe in him."

³⁷"You have seen him," Jesus said, "and he is speaking to you!"

³⁸"Yes, Lord, I believe!" the man said. And he worshiped Jesus.

³⁹Then Jesus told him, "I entered this world to render judgment—to

give sight to the blind and to show those who think they see that they are blind."

⁴⁰Some Pharisees who were standing nearby heard him and asked, "Are you saying we're blind?"

⁴¹"If you were blind, you wouldn't be guilty," Jesus replied. "But you remain guilty because you claim you can see.

What question did Jesus ask this man in verse 35?

How did the man respond to Jesus in verse 38?

Why did Jesus say He came into this world in verse 39?

DAY TEN

John 10.1-42 (NLT)

Shepherds have a deep love for their sheep. They lead them, protect them, feed them and care for them. Today you are going to read some of the most heart-warming and tender words of Jesus. They reveal how He feels about you and what He wants from you. Ask God to open your heart to receive what Jesus has to say today.

The Good Shepherd and His Sheep

¹"I tell you the truth, anyone who sneaks over the wall of a sheepfold, rather than going through the gate, must surely be a thief and a robber! ²But the one who enters through the gate is the shepherd of the sheep.

SHEEPFOLD:
In ancient Israel, shepherds would often put their flocks together overnight in a circular stone corral with one gate. The next morning each shepherd would stand at the gate and call to his sheep, and his sheep would come to him and follow him into the pasture.

³The gatekeeper opens the gate for him, and the sheep recognize his voice and come to him. He calls his own sheep by name and leads them out. ⁴After he has gathered his own flock, he walks ahead of them, and they follow him because they know his voice. ⁵They won't follow a stranger; they will run from him because they don't know his voice."

⁶Those who heard Jesus use this illustration didn't understand what he meant, ⁷so he explained it to them: "I tell you the truth, I am the gate for the sheep. ⁸All who came before me were thieves and robbers. But the true sheep did not listen to them. ⁹Yes, I am the gate. Those who come in through me will be saved. They will come and go freely and will find good pastures. ¹⁰The thief's purpose is to steal and kill and destroy. My purpose is to give them a rich and satisfying life.

¹¹"I am the good shepherd. The good shepherd sacrifices his life for the sheep. ¹²A hired hand will run when he sees a wolf coming. He will abandon the sheep because they don't belong to him and he isn't their shepherd. And so the wolf attacks them and scatters the flock. ¹³The hired hand runs away because he's working only for the money and doesn't really care about the sheep.

¹⁴"I am the good shepherd; I know my own sheep, and they know me, ¹⁵just as my Father knows me and I know the Father. So I sacrifice my life for the sheep. ¹⁶I have other sheep, too, that are not in this sheepfold. I must bring them also. They will listen to my voice, and there will be one flock with one shepherd.

¹⁷"The Father loves me because I sacrifice my life so I may take it back again. ¹⁸No one can take my life from me. I sacrifice it voluntarily. For I have the authority to lay it down when I want to and also to take it up again. For this is what my Father has commanded."

¹⁹When he said these things, the people were again divided in their opinions about him. ²⁰Some said, "He's demon possessed and out of his mind. Why listen to a man like that?" ²¹Others said, "This doesn't sound like a man possessed by a demon! Can a demon open the eyes of the blind?"

Jesus Claims to Be the Son of God

22It was now winter, and Jesus was in Jerusalem at the time of Hanukkah, the Festival of Dedication. **23**He was in the Temple, walking through the section known as Solomon's Colonnade. **24**The people surrounded him and asked, "How long are you going to keep us in suspense? If you are the Messiah, tell us plainly."

25Jesus replied, "I have already told you, and you don't believe me. The proof is the work I do in my Father's name. **26**But you don't believe me because you are not my sheep. **27**My sheep listen to my voice; I know them, and they follow me. **28**I give them eternal life, and they will never perish. No one can snatch them away from me, **29**for my Father has given them to me, and he is more powerful than anyone else. No one can snatch them from the Father's hand. **30**The Father and I are one."

31Once again the people picked up stones to kill him. **32**Jesus said, "At my Father's direction I have done many good works. For which one are you going to stone me?"

33They replied, "We're stoning you not for any good work, but for blasphemy! You, a mere man, claim to be God."

34Jesus replied, "It is written in your own Scriptures that God said to certain leaders of the people, 'I say, you are gods!' **35**And you know that the Scriptures cannot be altered. So if those people who received God's message were called 'gods,' **36**why do you call it blasphemy when I say, 'I am the Son of God'? After all, the Father set me apart and sent me into the world. **37**Don't believe me unless I carry out my Father's work. **38**But if I do his work, believe in the evidence of the miraculous works I have done, even if you don't believe me. Then you will know and understand that the Father is in me, and I am in the Father."

39Once again they tried to arrest him, but he got away and left them. **40**He went beyond the Jordan River near the place *where John was first baptizing and stayed there awhile. ⁴¹And many followed him. "John didn't perform miraculous signs," they remarked to one another, "but everything he said about this man has come true." ⁴²And many who were there believed in Jesus.*

What does Jesus reveal about Himself in verses 6-10?

_____
_____
_____
_____
_____

What does Jesus reveal about Himself in verses 14-15?

_____
_____
_____
_____
_____

What is Jesus referring to when He speaks about giving His life for the sheep in verses 17-18? _____

_____
_____
_____
_____

What wonderful promise does Jesus give in verses 27-30?

Why did the religious leaders react to Jesus so violently according to verses 31-33?

How did the common people respond to Jesus in verses 41-42?

DAY 11

John 11.1-57 (NLT)

Congratulations! You have made it halfway through your 21-day journey. Already you have learned so much about Jesus, but today you are going to get a front row seat to one of the most powerful moments in Jesus' life. Jesus stepped right into the middle of a grieving family and demonstrated His heart and His power. For many of the people that day, this was a turning point in their understanding of Jesus. Maybe today will be a turning point in your life, too.

The Raising of Lazarus

¹A man named Lazarus was sick. He lived in Bethany with his sisters, Mary and Martha. ²This is the Mary who later poured the expensive perfume on the Lord's feet and wiped them with her hair. Her brother, Lazarus, was sick. ³So the two sisters sent a message to Jesus telling him, "Lord, your dear friend is very sick."

⁴But when Jesus heard about it he said, "Lazarus's sickness will not end in death. No, it happened for the glory of God so that the Son of God will receive glory from this." ⁵So although Jesus loved Martha, Mary, and Lazarus, ⁶he stayed where he was for the next two days. ⁷Finally, he said to his disciples, "Let's go back to Judea." ⁸But his disciples objected. "Rabbi," they said, "only a few days ago the people in Judea were trying to stone you. Are you going there again?"

⁹Jesus replied, "There are twelve hours of daylight every day. During the day people can walk safely. They can see because they have the light of this world. ¹⁰But at night there is danger of stumbling because they have no light." ¹¹Then he said, "Our friend Lazarus has fallen asleep, but now I will go and wake him up."

¹²The disciples said, "Lord, if he is sleeping, he will soon get better!" ¹³They thought Jesus meant Lazarus was simply sleeping, but Jesus meant Lazarus had died.

¹⁴So he told them plainly, "Lazarus is dead. ¹⁵And for your sakes, I'm glad I wasn't there, for now you will really believe. Come, let's go see him."

¹⁶Thomas, nicknamed the Twin, said to his fellow disciples, "Let's go, too—and die with Jesus."

¹⁷When Jesus arrived at Bethany, he was told that Lazarus had already been in his grave for four days. ¹⁸Bethany was only a few miles down the road from Jerusalem, ¹⁹and many of the people had come to console Martha and Mary in their loss. ²⁰When Martha got word that Jesus was coming, she went to meet him. But Mary stayed in the house. ²¹Martha said to Jesus, "Lord, if only you had been here, my brother would not have died. ²²But even now I know that God will give you whatever you ask."

²³Jesus told her, "Your brother will rise again."

²⁴"Yes," Martha said, "he will rise when everyone else rises, at the last day."

²⁵Jesus told her, "I am the resurrection and the life. Anyone who believes in me will live, even after dying. ²⁶Everyone who lives in me and believes in me will never ever die. Do you believe this, Martha?"

²⁷"Yes, Lord," she told him. "I have always believed you are the Messiah, the Son of God, the one who has come into the world from God." ²⁸Then she returned to Mary. She called Mary aside

from the mourners and told her, "The Teacher is here and wants to see you." **29**So Mary immediately went to him.

30Jesus had stayed outside the village, at the place where Martha met him. **31**When the people who were at the house consoling Mary saw her leave so hastily, they assumed she was going to Lazarus's grave to weep. So they followed her there. **32**When Mary arrived and saw Jesus, she fell at his feet and said, "Lord, if only you had been here, my brother would not have died."

33When Jesus saw her weeping and saw the other people wailing with her, a deep anger welled up within him, and he was deeply troubled. **34**"Where have you put him?" he asked them.

They told him, "Lord, come and see." **35**Then Jesus wept. **36**The people who were standing nearby said, "See how much he loved him!" **37**But some said, "This man healed a blind man. Couldn't he have kept Lazarus from dying?"

38Jesus was still angry as he arrived at the tomb, a cave with a stone rolled across its entrance. **39**"Roll the stone aside," Jesus told them.

But Martha, the dead man's sister, protested, "Lord, he has been dead for four days. The smell will be terrible."

40Jesus responded, "Didn't I tell you that you would see God's glory if you believe?" **41**So they rolled the stone aside. Then Jesus looked up to heaven and said, "Father, thank you for hearing me. **42**You always hear me, but I said it out loud for the sake of all these people standing here, so that they will believe you sent me."

43Then Jesus shouted, "Lazarus, come out!" **44**And the dead man came out, his hands and feet bound in graveclothes, his face wrapped in a headcloth. Jesus told them, "Unwrap him and let him go!"

The Plot to Kill Jesus

⁴⁵*Many of the people who were with Mary believed in Jesus when they saw this happen.* ⁴⁶*But some went to the Pharisees and told them what Jesus had done.* ⁴⁷*Then the leading priests and Pharisees called the high council together. "What are we going to do?" they asked each other. "This man certainly performs many miraculous signs.* ⁴⁸*If we allow him to go on like this, soon everyone will believe in him. Then the Roman army will come and destroy both our Temple and our nation."*

⁴⁹*Caiaphas, who was high priest at that time, said, "You don't know what you're talking about!* ⁵⁰*You don't realize that it's better for you that one man should die for the people than for the whole nation to be destroyed."*

⁵¹*He did not say this on his own; as high priest at that time he was led to prophesy that Jesus would die for the entire nation.* ⁵²*And not only for that nation, but to bring together and unite all the children of God scattered around the world.*

⁵³*So from that time on, the Jewish leaders began to plot Jesus' death.* ⁵⁴*As a result, Jesus stopped his public ministry among the people and left Jerusalem. He went to a place near the wilderness, to the village of Ephraim, and stayed there with his disciples.*

⁵⁵*It was now almost time for the Jewish Passover celebration, and many people from all over the country arrived in Jerusalem several days early so they could go through the purification ceremony before Passover began.* ⁵⁶*They kept looking for Jesus, but as they stood around in the Temple, they said to each other, "What do you think? He won't come for Passover, will he?"* ⁵⁷*Meanwhile, the leading priests and Pharisees had publicly ordered that anyone seeing Jesus must report it immediately so they could arrest him.*

Why do you think Jesus delayed two extra days before going to see Mary, Martha and Lazarus in verse 6?

_____

_____

_____

_____

What did Jesus promise Martha in verses 25-26?

_____

_____

_____

_____

How did Martha respond to Jesus' promise in verse 27?

_____

_____

_____

_____

Why did Jesus weep in verse 35? _____

_____

_____

_____

_____

_____

How did the people respond to Jesus' demonstration of power in verses 45 and 53? _____

_____

_____

_____

_____

_____

_____

_____

_____

What stands out the most to you about Jesus in this passage?

_____

_____

_____

_____

_____

_____

_____

_____

_____

DAY 12

John 12.1-50 (NLT)

People's actions don't always match their true inner feelings. Sometimes a person will be nice to you in person, but then speak badly about you behind your back. Jesus experienced this firsthand. At this point in His ministry, Jesus was extremely popular. Massive crowds gathered to get a glimpse of Him and praised Him publicly, but many in their hearts did not truly believe He was who He claimed to be. In spite of it all, Jesus knew that He was headed back into Jerusalem for the last time. He would soon give His life to save those who would believe in Him.

Jesus Anointed at Bethany

*1Six days before the Passover celebration began, Jesus arrived in Bethany, the home of Lazarus—the man he had raised from the dead. 2A dinner was prepared in Jesus' honor. Martha served, and Lazarus was among those who ate with him. 3Then Mary took a twelve-ounce jar of expensive perfume made from essence of nard, and she anointed Jesus' feet with it, wiping his feet with her hair. The house was filled with the fragrance.
4But Judas Iscariot, the disciple who would soon betray him, said, 5"That perfume was worth a year's wages. It should have been sold and the money given to the poor." 6Not that he cared for the poor—he was a thief, and since he was in charge of the disciples' money, he often stole some for himself.*

⁷Jesus replied, "Leave her alone. She did this in preparation for my burial. ⁸You will always have the poor among you, but you will not always have me."
⁹When all the people heard of Jesus' arrival, they flocked to see him and also to see Lazarus, the man Jesus had raised from the dead. ¹⁰Then the leading priests decided to kill Lazarus, too, ¹¹for it was because of him that many of the people had deserted them and believed in Jesus.

Jesus' Triumphant Entry
¹²The next day, the news that Jesus was on the way to Jerusalem swept through the city. A large crowd of Passover visitors ¹³took palm branches and went down the road to meet him. They shouted, "Praise God!

WAVING PALM BRANCHES:
In ancient times people waved palm branches before conquering kings or political figures. In many ways, the people were praising Jesus as the one who would come and lead Israel back to the glory days of political strength and military power. But Jesus didn't come to establish an earthly kingdom, he came to bring God's kingdom to earth and make a way for sinful people to be made right with God.

Blessings on the one who comes in the name of the Lord!
Hail to the King of Israel!"
¹⁴Jesus found a young donkey and rode on it, fulfilling the prophecy that said:
¹⁵"Don't be afraid, people of Jerusalem.
Look, your King is coming,

riding on a donkey's colt."

16His disciples didn't understand at the time that this was a fulfillment of prophecy. But after Jesus entered into his glory, they remembered what had happened and realized that these things had been written about him.

17Many in the crowd had seen Jesus call Lazarus from the tomb, raising him from the dead, and they were telling others about it. **18**That was the reason so many went out to meet him—because they had heard about this miraculous sign. **19**Then the Pharisees said to each other, "There's nothing we can do. Look, everyone has gone after him!"

Jesus Predicts His Death

20Some Greeks who had come to Jerusalem for the Passover celebration **21**paid a visit to Philip, who was from Bethsaida in Galilee. They said, "Sir, we want to meet Jesus." **22**Philip told Andrew about it, and they went together to ask Jesus.

23Jesus replied, "Now the time has come for the Son of Man to enter into his glory. **24**I tell you the truth, unless a kernel of wheat is planted in the soil and dies, it remains alone. But its death will produce many new kernels—a plentiful harvest of new lives. **25**Those who love their life in this world will lose it. Those who care nothing for their life in this world will keep it for eternity. **26**Anyone who wants to serve me must follow me, because my servants must be where I am. And the Father will honor anyone who serves me.

27"Now my soul is deeply troubled. Should I pray, 'Father, save me from this hour'? But this is the very reason I came! **28**Father, bring glory to your name."

Then a voice spoke from heaven, saying, "I have already brought glory to my name, and I will do so again." **29**When the *crowd heard the voice, some thought it was thunder, while others declared an angel had spoken to him.*

30Then Jesus told them, "The voice was for your benefit, not mine. 31The time for judging this world has come, when Satan, the ruler of this world, will be cast out. 32And when I am lifted up from the earth, I will draw everyone to myself." 33He said this to indicate how he was going to die.

34The crowd responded, "We understood from Scripture that the Messiah would live forever. How can you say the Son of Man will die? Just who is this Son of Man, anyway?"

35Jesus replied, "My light will shine for you just a little longer. Walk in the light while you can, so the darkness will not overtake you. Those who walk in the darkness cannot see where they are going. 36Put your trust in the light while there is still time; then you will become children of the light."

After saying these things, Jesus went away and was hidden from them.

The Unbelief of the People

37But despite all the miraculous signs Jesus had done, most of the people still did not believe in him. 38This is exactly what Isaiah the prophet had predicted:

"Lord, who has believed our message?
   To whom has the Lord revealed his powerful arm?"

39But the people couldn't believe, for as Isaiah also said,
40"The Lord has blinded their eyes
   and hardened their hearts—
so that their eyes cannot see,
   and their hearts cannot understand,
and they cannot turn to me
   and have me heal them."

41Isaiah was referring to Jesus when he said this, because he saw the future and spoke of the Messiah's glory. **⁴²**Many people did believe in him, however, including some of the Jewish leaders. But they wouldn't admit it for fear that the Pharisees would expel them from the synagogue. **⁴³**For they loved human praise more than the praise of God.

⁴⁴Jesus shouted to the crowds, "If you trust me, you are trusting not only me, but also God who sent me. **⁴⁵**For when you see me, you are seeing the one who sent me. **⁴⁶**I have come as a light to shine in this dark world, so that all who put their trust in me will no longer remain in the dark. **⁴⁷**I will not judge those who hear me but don't obey me, for I have come to save the world and not to judge it. **⁴⁸**But all who reject me and my message will be judged on the day of judgment by the truth I have spoken. **⁴⁹** I don't speak on my own authority. The Father who sent me has commanded me what to say and how to say it. **⁵⁰**And I know his commands lead to eternal life; so I say whatever the Father tells me to say."

Why do you think Mary made such an extravagant gesture toward Jesus in verse 3? _____

_____

_____

_____

How do you think we should respond to Jesus for all that He has done for us? _____

_____

_____

What did Jesus mean when He spoke of a kernel of wheat dying and yet producing a harvest in verses 23-24?

_____

_____

_____

_____

How did God the Father respond to Jesus' faithfulness to go to Jerusalem and die in verses 27-29? _____

_____

_____

_____

What did Jesus say about those who believe in Him in verse 46?

_____

_____

_____

_____

What warning did Jesus give in verse 48? _____

_____

_____

_____

_____

_____

DAY 13

John 13.1-38 (NLT)

The next several readings all take place on the night before Jesus was arrested. He gathered with His closest friends in an upper room to share the Passover Meal together before His death. As He sits at the table, Jesus is troubled in His heart. He knows that one of His own men will betray Him into the hands of His enemies. At the same time He is filled with love for these men with whom He poured His life into for over three years. On this night Jesus gives His last commands to His faithful followers.

Jesus Washes His Disciples' Feet

¹Before the Passover celebration, Jesus knew that his hour had come to leave this world and return to his Father. He had loved his disciples during his ministry on earth, and now he loved them to the very end.

PASSOVER CELEBRATION:
The Passover is one of the greatest festivals in Israel, a time of remembrance of how God delivered His people from slavery in Egypt. God instructed the people to sacrifice a lamb and place its blood on the doorpost of their homes, so that when the angel of death saw the blood, divine judgment would "pass over" that home. Jesus was about to become the ultimate Passover Lamb, offering His life on the cross so that by His sacrifice God's wrath would pass over all who believe and trust in Him.

²It was time for supper, and the devil had already prompted Judas, son of Simon Iscariot, to betray Jesus. ³Jesus knew that the Father had given him authority over everything and that he had come from God and would return to God. ⁴So he got up from the table, took off his robe, wrapped a towel around his waist, ⁵and poured water into a basin. Then he began to wash the disciples' feet, drying them with the towel he had around him.

⁶When Jesus came to Simon Peter, Peter said to him, "Lord, are you going to wash my feet?"

⁷Jesus replied, "You don't understand now what I am doing, but someday you will."

⁸"No," Peter protested, "you will never ever wash my feet!"
Jesus replied, "Unless I wash you, you won't belong to me."

⁹Simon Peter exclaimed, "Then wash my hands and head as well, Lord, not just my feet!"

¹⁰Jesus replied, "A person who has bathed all over does not need to wash, except for the feet, to be entirely clean. And you disciples are clean, but not all of you." ¹¹For Jesus knew who would betray him. That is what he meant when he said, "Not all of you are clean."

¹²After washing their feet, he put on his robe again and sat down and asked, "Do you understand what I was doing?

¹³You call me 'Teacher' and 'Lord,' and you are right, because that's what I am. ¹⁴And since I, your Lord and Teacher, have washed your feet, you ought to wash each other's feet. ¹⁵I have given you an example to follow. Do as I have done to you. ¹⁶I tell you the truth, slaves are not greater than their master. Nor is the messenger more important than the one who sends the message. ¹⁷Now that you know these things, God will bless you for doing them.

Jesus Predicts His Betrayal

¹⁸"I am not saying these things to all of you; I know the ones I have chosen. But this fulfills the Scripture that says, 'The one who eats my food has turned against me.' ¹⁹I tell you this beforehand, so that when it happens you will believe that I am the Messiah. ²⁰I tell you the truth, anyone who welcomes my messenger is welcoming me, and anyone who welcomes me is welcoming the Father who sent me."

²¹Now Jesus was deeply troubled, and he exclaimed, "I tell you the truth, one of you will betray me!"

²²The disciples looked at each other, wondering whom he could mean. ²³The disciple Jesus loved was sitting next to Jesus at the table. ²⁴Simon Peter motioned to him to ask, "Who's he talking about?" ²⁵So that disciple leaned over to Jesus and asked, "Lord, who is it?"

²⁶Jesus responded, "It is the one to whom I give the bread I dip in the bowl." And when he had dipped it, he gave it to Judas, son of Simon Iscariot. ²⁷When Judas had eaten the bread, Satan entered into him. Then Jesus told him, "Hurry and do what you're going to do." ²⁸None of the others at the table knew what Jesus meant. ²⁹Since Judas was their treasurer, some thought Jesus was telling him to go and pay for the food or to give some money to the poor. ³⁰So Judas left at once, going out into the night.

Jesus Predicts Peter's Denial

³¹As soon as Judas left the room, Jesus said, "The time has come for the Son of Man to enter into his glory, and God will be glorified because of him. ³²And since God receives glory because of the Son, he will give his own glory to the Son, and he will do so at once. ³³Dear children, I will be with you only a little longer. And as I told the Jewish leaders, you will search for

me, but you can't come where I am going. ³⁴So now I am giving you a new commandment: Love each other. Just as I have loved you, you should love each other. ³⁵Your love for one another will prove to the world that you are my disciples."

³⁶Simon Peter asked, "Lord, where are you going?"

And Jesus replied, "You can't go with me now, but you will follow me later."

³⁷"But why can't I come now, Lord?" he asked. "I'm ready to die for you."

³⁸Jesus answered, "Die for me? I tell you the truth, Peter—before the rooster crows tomorrow morning, you will deny three times that you even know me.

Why did Jesus wash His disciples' feet according to verses 12-15?

_____
_____
_____
_____
_____
_____
_____
_____
_____
_____
_____
_____
_____

What new command did Jesus give His disciples in verse 34?

_____
_____
_____
_____

Who is about to betray Jesus in verses 21, 26-27?

_____
_____
_____
_____

Who is about to deny Jesus in verse 38?

_____
_____
_____
_____
_____
_____
_____

DAY 14

John 14.1-31 (NLT)

Final words matter. On this last night, Jesus shares His final words with the men He has loved and led for over three years. Judas leaves the room to begin his work of betrayal and Jesus leans in to make some powerful promises to His disciples. These promises still belong to all who trust and follow Jesus.

Jesus, the Way to the Father
¹"Don't let your hearts be troubled. Trust in God, and trust also in me. ²There is more than enough room in my Father's home. If this were not so, would I have told you that I am going to prepare a place for you? ³When everything is ready, I will come and get you, so that you will always be with me where I am. ⁴And you know the way to where I am going."
⁵"No, we don't know, Lord," Thomas said. "We have no idea where you are going, so how can we know the way?"
⁶Jesus told him, "I am the way, the truth, and the life. No one can come to the Father except through me. ⁷If you had really known me, you would know who my Father is. From now on, you do know him and have seen him!"
⁸Philip said, "Lord, show us the Father, and we will be satisfied."
⁹ Jesus replied, "Have I been with you all this time, Philip, and yet you still don't know who I am? Anyone who has seen me has seen

the Father! So why are you asking me to show him to you? **¹⁰**Don't you believe that I am in the Father and the Father is in me? The words I speak are not my own, but my Father who lives in me does his work through me. **¹¹**Just believe that I am in the Father and the Father is in me. Or at least believe because of the work you have seen me do.

¹²"I tell you the truth, anyone who believes in me will do the same works I have done, and even greater works, because I am going to be with the Father. **¹³**You can ask for anything in my name, and I will do it, so that the Son can bring glory to the Father. **¹⁴**Yes, ask me for anything in my name, and I will do it!

Jesus Promises the Holy Spirit

¹⁵"If you love me, obey my commandments. **¹⁶**And I will ask the Father, and he will give you another Advocate, who will never leave you. **¹⁷**He is the Holy Spirit, who leads into all truth. The world cannot receive him, because it isn't looking for him and doesn't recognize him. But you know him, because he lives with you now and later will be in you.

THE HOLY SPIRIT:

The Holy Spirit is the third person of the Trinity – God the Father, Jesus the Son and the Holy Spirit. The Holy Spirit is the very person and presence of God who comes to dwell in all who believe and follow Jesus.

¹⁸ No, I will not abandon you as orphans—I will come to you. ¹⁹ Soon the world will no longer see me, but you will see me. Since I live, you also will live. ²⁰ When I am raised to life again, you will know that I am in my Father, and you are in me, and I am in you. ²¹ Those who accept my commandments and obey them are the ones who love me. And because they love me, my Father will love them. And I will love them and reveal myself to each of them."

²² Judas (not Judas Iscariot, but the other disciple with that name) said to him, "Lord, why are you going to reveal yourself only to us and not to the world at large?"

²³ Jesus replied, "All who love me will do what I say. My Father will love them, and we will come and make our home with each of them. ²⁴ Anyone who doesn't love me will not obey me. And remember, my words are not my own. What I am telling you is from the Father who sent me. ²⁵ I am telling you these things now while I am still with you.

²⁶ But when the Father sends the Advocate as my representative—that is, the Holy Spirit—he will teach you everything and will remind you of everything I have told you.

²⁷ "I am leaving you with a gift—peace of mind and heart. And the peace I give is a gift the world cannot give. So don't be troubled or afraid. ²⁸ Remember what I told you: I am going away, but I will come back to you again. If you really loved me, you would be happy that I am going to the Father, who is greater than I am. ²⁹ I have told you these things before they happen so that when they do happen, you will believe.

30 "I don't have much more time to talk to you, because the ruler of this world approaches. He has no power over me, **31** but I will do what the Father requires of me, so that the world will know that I love the Father. Come, let's be going.

What promise did Jesus give His followers in verses 1-4?

_____

_____

_____

What very important statement did Jesus make about Himself in verse 6?

_____

_____

How does a person show their love for God according to verses 15 and 23?

_____

_____

_____

What do you learn about the Holy Spirit from verses 16-17?

_____

_____

_____

What gift does Jesus leave for those who love Him in verse 27?

_____

_____

What stands out the most to you from what Jesus said in this passage?

_____

_____

DAY 15

John 15.1-27 (NLT)

Have you ever walked through a vineyard? The trunk of the vine is large and strong coming out of the ground. The branches run along the trellis where large clusters of ripe grapes are proudly displayed. The only way the branches can bear fruit is if they stay vitally connected to the vine. If they are cut off, they will just wither and die. Jesus uses this illustration to speak about how we need to stay vitally connected to Him so that we can live fruitful lives.

Jesus, the True Vine

1"I am the true grapevine, and my Father is the gardener. 2He cuts off every branch of mine that doesn't produce fruit, and he prunes the branches that do bear fruit so they will produce even more. 3You have already been pruned and purified by the message I have given you. 4Remain in me, and I will remain in you. For a branch cannot produce fruit if it is severed from the vine, and you cannot be fruitful unless you remain in me.
5"Yes, I am the vine; you are the branches. Those who remain in me, and I in them, will produce much fruit. For apart from me you can do nothing. 6Anyone who does not remain in me is thrown away like a useless branch and withers. Such branches are gathered into a pile to be burned. 7But if you remain in me and my words remain in you, you may ask for anything you want, and it

will be granted! **⁸**When you produce much fruit, you are my true disciples. This brings great glory to my Father.

⁹"I have loved you even as the Father has loved me. Remain in my love. **¹⁰**When you obey my commandments, you remain in my love, just as I obey my Father's commandments and remain in his love. **¹¹**I have told you these things so that you will be filled with my joy. Yes, your joy will overflow! **¹²**This is my commandment: Love each other in the same way I have loved you. **¹³**There is no greater love than to lay down one's life for one's friends. **¹⁴**You are my friends if you do what I command. **¹⁵**I no longer call you slaves, because a master doesn't confide in his slaves. Now you are my friends, since I have told you everything the Father told me. **¹⁶**You didn't choose me. I chose you. I appointed you to go and produce lasting fruit, so that the Father will give you whatever you ask for, using my name. **¹⁷**This is my command: Love each other.

The World's Hatred

¹⁸"If the world hates you, remember that it hated me first. **¹⁹**The world would love you as one of its own if you belonged to it, but you are no longer part of the world. I chose you to come out of the world, so it hates you. **²⁰**Do you remember what I told you? 'A slave is not greater than the master.' Since they persecuted me, naturally they will persecute you. And if they had listened to me, they would listen to you. **²¹**They will do all this to you because of me, for they have rejected the one who sent me. **²²**They would not be guilty if I had not come and spoken to them. But now they have no excuse for their sin. **²³**Anyone who hates me also hates my Father. **²⁴**If I hadn't done such miraculous signs among them that no one else could do, they would not be guilty. But as it is, they have seen everything I did, yet they still hate me and my Father. **²⁵**This fulfills what is written in their Scriptures: 'They hated *me without cause.'*

²⁶"But I will send you the Advocate—the Spirit of truth. He will come to you from the Father and will testify all about me. ²⁷And you must also testify about me because you have been with me from the beginning of my ministry.

Look carefully at verse 5. What do you think it means to remain in Jesus?

_____
_____
_____
_____
_____

What does Jesus promise if you remain in Him?

_____
_____
_____
_____

What can we do apart from Jesus?

_____
_____
_____
_____

If you follow Jesus, what kind of treatment from this world can you expect according to verses 18-19?

What would it look like for you to remain in Jesus and make Him the center of your life?

DAY 16

John 16.1-33 (NLT)

Imagine someone you love telling you that you won't ever see them again. How would you feel? Sad? Abandoned? Alone? As Jesus was telling His men that He was about to suffer and die, His followers felt all the same emotions. How could Jesus just abandon them like this? How could He leave them in their sorrow? But Jesus makes it clear He is not abandoning them. He is leaving behind the Holy Spirit who will lead them and empower them. Yes, they are sad now, but soon they will be filled with joy!

¹"I have told you these things so that you won't abandon your faith. ²For you will be expelled from the synagogues, and the time is coming when those who kill you will think they are doing a holy service for God. ³This is because they have never known the Father or me. ⁴Yes, I'm telling you these things now, so that when they happen, you will remember my warning. I didn't tell you earlier because I was going to be with you for a while longer.

The Work of the Holy Spirit
⁵"But now I am going away to the one who sent me, and not one of you is asking where I am going. ⁶Instead, you grieve because of what I've told you. ⁷But in fact, it is best for you that I go away,

because if I don't, the Advocate won't come. If I do go away, then I will send him to you. **⁸**And when he comes, he will convict the world of its sin, and of God's righteousness, and of the coming judgment. **⁹**The world's sin is that it refuses to believe in me. **¹⁰**Righteousness is available because I go to the Father, and you will see me no more. **¹¹**Judgment will come because the ruler of this world has already been judged.

¹²"There is so much more I want to tell you, but you can't bear it now. **¹³**When the Spirit of truth comes, he will guide you into all truth. He will not speak on his own but will tell you what he has heard. He will tell you about the future. **¹⁴**He will bring me glory by telling you whatever he receives from me. **¹⁵**All that belongs to the Father is mine; this is why I said, 'The Spirit will tell you whatever he receives from me.'

Sadness Will Be Turned to Joy

¹⁶"In a little while you won't see me anymore. But a little while after that, you will see me again."

¹⁷Some of the disciples asked each other, "What does he mean when he says, 'In a little while you won't see me, but then you will see me,' and 'I am going to the Father'? **¹⁸**And what does he mean by 'a little while'? We don't understand."

¹⁹Jesus realized they wanted to ask him about it, so he said, "Are you asking yourselves what I meant? I said in a little while you won't see me, but a little while after that you will see me again. **²⁰**I tell you the truth, you will weep and mourn over what is going to happen to me, but the world will rejoice. You will grieve, but your grief will suddenly turn to wonderful joy. **²¹**It will be like a woman suffering the pains of labor. When her child is born, her anguish gives way to joy because she has brought a new baby into the world. **²²**So you have sorrow now, but I will see you again;

then you will rejoice, and no one can rob you of that joy. **23***At that time you won't need to ask me for anything. I tell you the truth, you will ask the Father directly, and he will grant your request because you use my name.* **24***You haven't done this before. Ask, using my name, and you will receive, and you will have abundant joy.*

25*"I have spoken of these matters in figures of speech, but soon I will stop speaking figuratively and will tell you plainly all about the Father.* **26***Then you will ask in my name. I'm not saying I will ask the Father on your behalf,* **27***for the Father himself loves you dearly because you love me and believe that I came from God.* **28***Yes, I came from the Father into the world, and now I will leave the world and return to the Father."*

29*Then his disciples said, "At last you are speaking plainly and not figuratively.* **30***Now we understand that you know everything, and there's no need to question you. From this we believe that you came from God."*

31*Jesus asked, "Do you finally believe?* **32***But the time is coming—indeed it's here now—when you will be scattered, each one going his own way, leaving me alone. Yet I am not alone because the Father is with me.* **33***I have told you all this so that you may have peace in me. Here on earth you will have many trials and sorrows. But take heart, because I have overcome the world."*

What does the Holy Spirit do in the life of the believer according to verses 7-11 and 13-15? Make a short list.

_____
_____
_____
_____

What did Jesus say would happen to His disciples in verse 20?

_____
_____
_____
_____
_____

How does the Father feel about every follower of Jesus according to verse 27? _____

_____
_____
_____
_____
_____

When you face problems and trials in life, what promises does Jesus leave for you in verse 33? _____

_____
_____
_____
_____
_____
_____
_____
_____

DAY 17

John 17.1-26 (NLT)

Imagine what it would be like if you could listen to Jesus pray! In this section, John records the prayer of Jesus that night. As you read these words, think about how Jesus is praying for His disciples. Keep in mind that Jesus is praying for you, too! This is the last section that describes Jesus' time with His men before His death.

The Prayer of Jesus

¹After saying all these things, Jesus looked up to heaven and said, "Father, the hour has come. Glorify your Son so he can give glory back to you. ²For you have given him authority over everyone. He gives eternal life to each one you have given him. ³And this is the way to have eternal life—to know you, the only true God, and Jesus Christ, the one you sent to earth. ⁴I brought glory to you here on earth by completing the work you gave me to do. ⁵Now, Father, bring me into the glory we shared before the world began. ⁶"I have revealed you to the ones you gave me from this world. They were always yours. You gave them to me, and they have kept your word. ⁷Now they know that everything I have is a gift from you, ⁸for I have passed on to them the message you gave me. They accepted it and know that I came from you, and they believe you sent me.

⁹"My prayer is not for the world, but for those you have given me, because they belong to you. ¹⁰All who are mine belong to you, and you have given them to me, so they bring me glory. ¹¹Now I am departing from the world; they are staying in this world, but I am coming to you. Holy Father, you have given me your name; now protect them by the power of your name so that they will be united just as we are. ¹²During my time here, I protected them by the power of the name you gave me. I guarded them so that not one was lost, except the one headed for destruction, as the Scriptures foretold.
¹³"Now I am coming to you. I told them many things while I was with them in this world so they would be filled with my joy. ¹⁴I have given them your word. And the world hates them because they do not belong to the world, just as I do not belong to the world. ¹⁵I'm not asking you to take them out of the world, but to keep them safe from the evil one. ¹⁶They do not belong to this world any more than I do. ¹⁷Make them holy by your truth; teach them your word, which is truth. ¹⁸Just as you sent me into the world, I am sending them into the world. ¹⁹And I give myself as a holy sacrifice for them so they can be made holy by your truth.
²⁰"I am praying not only for these disciples but also for all who will ever believe in me through their message. ²¹I pray that they will all be one, just as you and I are one—as you are in me, Father, and I am in you. And may they be in us so that the world will believe you sent me.
²²"I have given them the glory you gave me, so they may be one as we are one. ²³I am in them and you are in me. May they experience such perfect unity that the world will know that you sent me and that you love them as much as you love me. ²⁴Father, I want these whom you have given me to be with me where I am. Then they can see all the glory you gave me because you loved me even before the world began!
²⁵"O righteous Father, the world doesn't know you, but I do; and

these disciples know you sent me. ²⁶I have revealed you to them, and I will continue to do so. Then your love for me will be in them, and I will be in them."

How does Jesus describe the way to have eternal life in verse 3?
_____
_____
_____
_____
_____

What does verse 5 tell you about Jesus' relationship with His Father?
_____
_____
_____
_____
_____
_____

What did Jesus ask the Father to do for His disciples in verses 11, 13 and 17? _____
_____
_____
_____

Jesus also prayed for those who would believe because of the disciples' testimony about Jesus. That means Jesus is praying for you! What does Jesus ask His Father to do for you according to verse 21? _____

_____

_____

_____

_____

_____

Thinking about how Jesus prayed, how can you begin to pray for the people in your life?

_____

_____

_____

_____

_____

_____

_____

_____

_____

_____

_____

_____

DAY 18

John 18.1-40 (NLT)

It is so hard to watch when innocent people suffer. In this section you will see Jesus as He is arrested, tried, beaten, rejected and sentenced to death. As you read this account, think about how much Jesus must love you to endure such treatment.

Jesus Is Betrayed and Arrested

¹After saying these things, Jesus crossed the Kidron Valley with his disciples and entered a grove of olive trees. ²Judas, the betrayer, knew this place, because Jesus had often gone there with his disciples. ³The leading priests and Pharisees had given Judas a contingent of Roman soldiers and Temple guards to accompany him. Now with blazing torches, lanterns, and weapons, they arrived at the olive grove.
⁴Jesus fully realized all that was going to happen to him, so he stepped forward to meet them. "Who are you looking for?" he asked.
⁵"Jesus the Nazarene," they replied.
"I am he," Jesus said. (Judas, who betrayed him, was standing with them.) ⁶As Jesus said "I am he," they all drew back and fell to the ground! ⁷Once more he asked them, "Who are you looking for?" And again they replied, "Jesus the Nazarene."

⁸"I told you that I am he," Jesus said. "And since I am the one you want, let these others go." ⁹He did this to fulfill his own statement: "I did not lose a single one of those you have given me."
¹⁰Then Simon Peter drew a sword and slashed off the right ear of Malchus, the high priest's slave. ¹¹But Jesus said to Peter, "Put your sword back into its sheath. Shall I not drink from the cup of suffering the Father has given me?"

Jesus at the High Priest's House

¹²So the soldiers, their commanding officer, and the Temple guards arrested Jesus and tied him up. ¹³First they took him to Annas, since he was the father-in-law of Caiaphas, the high priest at that time.

THE TRIALS OF JESUS:

Jesus endured several illegal trials in the middle of the night. First, He was tried before Annas, the former High Priest of Israel. Then He was tried by Caiaphas, the ruling High Priest. Afterward Jesus was led to Pilate, the Roman Governor of Israel, where He was accused of sedition, claiming Himself to be a king.

¹⁴Caiaphas was the one who had told the other Jewish leaders, "It's better that one man should die for the people."

Peter's First Denial

¹⁵Simon Peter followed Jesus, as did another of the disciples. That other disciple was acquainted with the high priest, so he was allowed to enter the high priest's courtyard with Jesus. ¹⁶Peter had to stay outside the gate. Then the disciple who knew the high priest spoke to the woman watching at the gate, and she let Peter in.

¹⁷The woman asked Peter, "You're not one of that man's disciples, are you?"

"No," he said, "I am not."

¹⁸Because it was cold, the household servants and the guards had made a charcoal fire. They stood around it, warming themselves, and Peter stood with them, warming himself.

The High Priest Questions Jesus

¹⁹Inside, the high priest began asking Jesus about his followers and what he had been teaching them. ²⁰Jesus replied, "Everyone knows what I teach. I have preached regularly in the synagogues and the Temple, where the people gather. I have not spoken in secret. ²¹Why are you asking me this question? Ask those who heard me. They know what I said."

²²Then one of the Temple guards standing nearby slapped Jesus across the face. "Is that the way to answer the high priest?" he demanded.

²³Jesus replied, "If I said anything wrong, you must prove it. But if I'm speaking the truth, why are you beating me?"

²⁴Then Annas bound Jesus and sent him to Caiaphas, the high priest.

Peter's Second and Third Denials

²⁵Meanwhile, as Simon Peter was standing by the fire warming himself, they asked him again, "You're not one of his disciples, are you?"

He denied it, saying, "No, I am not."

²⁶But one of the household slaves of the high priest, a relative of the man whose ear Peter had cut off, asked, "Didn't I see you out there in the olive grove with Jesus?" ²⁷Again Peter denied it. And immediately a rooster crowed.

Jesus' Trial before Pilate

28 Jesus' trial before Caiaphas ended in the early hours of the morning. Then he was taken to the headquarters of the Roman governor. His accusers didn't go inside because it would defile them, and they wouldn't be allowed to celebrate the Passover. **29** So Pilate, the governor, went out to them and asked, "What is your charge against this man?"

30 "We wouldn't have handed him over to you if he weren't a criminal!" they retorted.

31 "Then take him away and judge him by your own law," Pilate told them.

"Only the Romans are permitted to execute someone," the Jewish leaders replied. **32** (This fulfilled Jesus' prediction about the way he would die.)

33 Then Pilate went back into his headquarters and called for Jesus to be brought to him. "Are you the king of the Jews?" he asked him.

34 Jesus replied, "Is this your own question, or did others tell you about me?"

35 "Am I a Jew?" Pilate retorted. "Your own people and their leading priests brought you to me for trial. Why? What have you done?"

36 Jesus answered, "My Kingdom is not an earthly kingdom. If it were, my followers would fight to keep me from being handed over to the Jewish leaders. But my Kingdom is not of this world."

37 Pilate said, "So you are a king?"

Jesus responded, "You say I am a king. Actually, I was born and came into the world to testify to the truth. All who love the truth recognize that what I say is true."

38 "What is truth?" Pilate asked. Then he went out again to the people and told them, "He is not guilty of any crime. **39** But you *have a custom of asking me to release one prisoner each year at Passover. Would you like me to release this 'King of the Jews'?"* ⁴⁰*But they shouted back, "No! Not this man. We want Barabbas!" (Barabbas was a revolutionary.)*

Looking in verse 27, while Jesus was being interrogated, Peter sat outside in the outer courtyard. Why do you think he was so quick to deny that he even knew Jesus?

Why did they take Jesus to Pilate according to verse 31?

After examining Jesus, how did Pilate rule in verse 38?

_____
_____
_____
_____
_____
_____
_____

When given a choice between Jesus or a dangerous revolutionary named Barabbas, who did the people choose? (see verse 40). Why did they make this choice?

_____
_____
_____
_____
_____
_____
_____
_____
_____
_____
_____
_____
_____
_____

DAY 19

John 19.1-42 (NLT)

We see crosses everywhere. Crosses sit on top of church steeples. People wear them as jewelry and adorn their walls with crosses. Some even have crosses tattooed on their bodies. But the cross of Jesus was anything but beautiful and decorative. In Jesus' day the cross was a terrible instrument of suffering and death inflicted on the worst of criminals. Yet Jesus went to the cross willingly. He embraced the cross so that He could pay the penalty for your sin, and make a way for you to find forgiveness and eternal life. Take time to slowly read through this section today. Think about what Jesus suffered for you and remember Jesus' words, *"There is no greater love than to lay down one's life for one's friends,"* **(John 15.13 NLT)**.

Jesus Sentenced to Death
¹Then Pilate had Jesus flogged with a lead-tipped whip. ²The soldiers wove a crown of thorns and put it on his head, and they put a purple robe on him. ³"Hail! King of the Jews!" they mocked, as they slapped him across the face.
⁴Pilate went outside again and said to the people, "I am going to bring him out to you now, but understand clearly that I find him not guilty." ⁵Then Jesus came out wearing the crown of thorns and the purple robe. And Pilate said, "Look, here is the man!"

⁶When they saw him, the leading priests and Temple guards began shouting, "Crucify him! Crucify him!"

"Take him yourselves and crucify him," Pilate said. "I find him not guilty."

⁷The Jewish leaders replied, "By our law he ought to die because he called himself the Son of God."

⁸When Pilate heard this, he was more frightened than ever. ⁹He took Jesus back into the headquarters again and asked him, "Where are you from?" But Jesus gave no answer. ¹⁰"Why don't you talk to me?" Pilate demanded. "Don't you realize that I have the power to release you or crucify you?"

¹¹Then Jesus said, "You would have no power over me at all unless it were given to you from above. So the one who handed me over to you has the greater sin."

¹²Then Pilate tried to release him, but the Jewish leaders shouted, "If you release this man, you are no 'friend of Caesar.' Anyone who declares himself a king is a rebel against Caesar."

¹³When they said this, Pilate brought Jesus out to them again. Then Pilate sat down on the judgment seat on the platform that is called the Stone Pavement (in Hebrew, Gabbatha). ¹⁴It was now about noon on the day of preparation for the Passover. And Pilate said to the people, "Look, here is your king!"

¹⁵"Away with him," they yelled. "Away with him! Crucify him!"

"What? Crucify your king?" Pilate asked.

"We have no king but Caesar," the leading priests shouted back.

¹⁶Then Pilate turned Jesus over to them to be crucified.

The Crucifixion

So they took Jesus away. ¹⁷Carrying the cross by himself, he went to the place called Place of the Skull (in Hebrew, Golgotha). ¹⁸There they nailed him to the cross. Two others were crucified with him, one on either side, with Jesus between them. ¹⁹And Pilate

posted a sign on the cross that read, "Jesus of Nazareth, the King of the Jews." **20**The place where Jesus was crucified was near the city, and the sign was written in Hebrew, Latin, and Greek, so that many people could read it.
21Then the leading priests objected and said to Pilate, "Change it from 'The King of the Jews' to 'He said, I am King of the Jews.'"
22Pilate replied, "No, what I have written, I have written."
23When the soldiers had crucified Jesus, they divided his clothes among the four of them. They also took his robe, but it was seamless, woven in one piece from top to bottom. **24**So they said, "Rather than tearing it apart, let's throw dice for it." This fulfilled the Scripture that says, "They divided my garments among themselves and threw dice for my clothing." So that is what they did.
25Standing near the cross were Jesus' mother, and his mother's sister, Mary (the wife of Clopas), and Mary Magdalene. **26**When Jesus saw his mother standing there beside the disciple he loved, he said to her, "Dear woman, here is your son." **27**And he said to this disciple, "Here is your mother." And from then on this disciple took her into his home.

The Death of Jesus

28Jesus knew that his mission was now finished, and to fulfill Scripture he said, "I am thirsty." **29**A jar of sour wine was sitting there, so they soaked a sponge in it, put it on a hyssop branch, and held it up to his lips. **30**When Jesus had tasted it, he said, "It is finished!" Then he bowed his head and gave up his spirit.

IT IS FINISHED:
It is finished: The last word Jesus cried out from the cross was *"tetelestai,"* which means, *"it is complete,"* or *"paid in full."* It was the same word merchants would stamp on an invoice that was completely paid.

31It was the day of preparation, and the Jewish leaders didn't want the bodies hanging there the next day, which was the Sabbath (and a very special Sabbath, because it was Passover week). So they asked Pilate to hasten their deaths by ordering that their legs be broken. Then their bodies could be taken down. **32**So the soldiers came and broke the legs of the two men crucified with Jesus. **33**But when they came to Jesus, they saw that he was already dead, so they didn't break his legs. **34**One of the soldiers, however, pierced his side with a spear, and immediately blood and water flowed out. **35**(This report is from an eyewitness giving an accurate account. He speaks the truth so that you also may continue to believe.) **36**These things happened in fulfillment of the Scriptures that say, "Not one of his bones will be broken," **37**and "They will look on the one they pierced."

The Burial of Jesus

38Afterward Joseph of Arimathea, who had been a secret disciple of Jesus (because he feared the Jewish leaders), asked Pilate for permission to take down Jesus' body. When Pilate gave permission, Joseph came and took the body away. **39**With him came Nicodemus, the man who had come to Jesus at night. He brought about seventy-five pounds of perfumed ointment made from myrrh and aloes. **40**Following Jewish burial custom, they wrapped Jesus' body with the spices in long sheets of linen cloth. **41**The place of crucifixion was near a garden, where there was a new tomb, never used before. **42**And so, because it was the day of preparation for the Jewish Passover and since the tomb was close at hand, they laid Jesus there.

Why did the Jewish leaders want Jesus to die according to verse 7?

_____
_____
_____
_____
_____
_____

A sign listing their crime was usually posted over the head of the person being crucified. **What was the crime Jesus committed according to verses 19-20?** _____

_____
_____
_____
_____
_____

Some have suggested that Jesus wasn't really dead when He was taken off the cross. ***Do you think there is any way Jesus could have survived the cross according to verses 34-35?***

_____
_____
_____
_____
_____

Remember Nicodemus from day three? Here he is taking a public stand for Jesus and caring for Jesus' body. **Where did they place Jesus' body according to verses 41-42?**

_____

_____

_____

_____

_____

_____

_____

What stands out the most to you from what you just read?

_____

_____

_____

_____

_____

_____

_____

_____

_____

_____

_____

_____

DAY 20

John 20.1-31 (NLT)

Everyone loves a comeback story. We love to cheer for athletes who are all washed up, but somehow fight their way back to the top. Today, however, is the greatest comeback story of all time! Jesus had predicted that He would die and that He would rise again. Before His death He told His disciples, *"I tell you the truth, you will weep and mourn over what is going to happen to me, but the world will rejoice. You will grieve, but your grief will suddenly turn to wonderful joy...so you will have sorrow now, but I will see you again; then you will rejoice and no one can rob you of that joy,"* **(John 16.20,22 NLT)**.

The resurrection of Jesus from the dead is what sets Jesus apart from every other religious leader. No one has ever died for the sins of mankind and come back to life – no one except Jesus. John gives a firsthand, eye-witness account of both Jesus' death and His resurrection from the dead. Today, ask God to show you the truth about Jesus as you read.

The Resurrection

¹*Early on Sunday morning, while it was still dark, Mary Magdalene came to the tomb and found that the stone had been rolled away from the entrance.* ²*She ran and found Simon*

THE OTHER DISCIPLE:
Who is this person? John, the author of this book often uses the phrases, *"the other disciple"* **(John 1.37; 18.15; 20.2-3)** or, *"the disciple Jesus loved"* **(John 13.23; 19.26; 21.7, 20)** as code words for himself.

Peter and the other disciple, the one whom Jesus loved. She said, "They have taken the Lord's body out of the tomb, and we don't know where they have put him!"

3 Peter and the other disciple started out for the tomb. **4** They were both running, but the other disciple outran Peter and reached the tomb first. **5** He stooped and looked in and saw the linen wrappings lying there, but he didn't go in. **6** Then Simon Peter arrived and went inside. He also noticed the linen wrappings lying there, **7** while the cloth that had covered Jesus' head was folded up and lying apart from the other wrappings. **8** Then the disciple who had reached the tomb first also went in, and he saw and believed— **9** for until then they still hadn't understood the Scriptures that said Jesus must rise from the dead. **10** Then they went home.

Jesus Appears to Mary Magdalene

11 Mary was standing outside the tomb crying, and as she wept, she stooped and looked in. **12** She saw two white-robed angels, one sitting at the head and the other at the foot of the place where the body of Jesus had been lying. **13** "Dear woman, why are you crying?" the angels asked her.

"Because they have taken away my Lord," she replied, "and I don't know where they have put him."

14 She turned to leave and saw someone standing there. It was Jesus, but she didn't recognize him. **15** "Dear woman, why are you crying?" Jesus asked her. "Who are you looking for?"

She thought he was the gardener. "Sir," she said, "if you have taken him away, tell me where you have put him, and I will go and get him."

16 "Mary!" Jesus said.

She turned to him and cried out, "Rabboni!" (which is Hebrew for "Teacher").

17"Don't cling to me," Jesus said, "for I haven't yet ascended to the Father. But go find my brothers and tell them, 'I am ascending to my Father and your Father, to my God and your God.'"
18Mary Magdalene found the disciples and told them, "I have seen the Lord!" Then she gave them his message.

Jesus Appears to His Disciples

19That Sunday evening the disciples were meeting behind locked doors because they were afraid of the Jewish leaders. Suddenly, Jesus was standing there among them! "Peace be with you," he said. **20**As he spoke, he showed them the wounds in his hands and his side. They were filled with joy when they saw the Lord! **21**Again he said, "Peace be with you. As the Father has sent me, so I am sending you." **22**Then he breathed on them and said, "Receive the Holy Spirit. **23**If you forgive anyone's sins, they are forgiven. If you do not forgive them, they are not forgiven."

Jesus Appears to Thomas

24One of the twelve disciples, Thomas (nicknamed the Twin), was not with the others when Jesus came. **25**They told him, "We have seen the Lord!"

But he replied, "I won't believe it unless I see the nail wounds in his hands, put my fingers into them, and place my hand into the wound in his side."

26Eight days later the disciples were together again, and this time Thomas was with them. The doors were locked; but suddenly, as before, Jesus was standing among them. "Peace be with you," he said. **27**Then he said to Thomas, "Put your finger here, and look at my hands. Put your hand into the wound in my side. Don't be faithless any longer. Believe!"

28"My Lord and my God!" Thomas exclaimed.

²⁹Then Jesus told him, "You believe because you have seen me. Blessed are those who believe without seeing me."

Purpose of the Book
³⁰The disciples saw Jesus do many other miraculous signs in addition to the ones recorded in this book. ³¹But these are written so that you may continue to believe that Jesus is the Messiah, the Son of God, and that by believing in him you will have life by the power of his name.

What did Peter and John see when they went into the empty tomb in verses 5-9?

_____

_____

_____

_____

Who was the first person to see Jesus alive according to verse 16?

_____

_____

How did Jesus first appear to His disciples in verses 19-20?

_____

_____

_____

_____

_____

What did Jesus tell Thomas, who struggled with doubt in verse 29?

_____

_____

_____

Why did John write this eye-witness account according to verses 30-31?

_____

_____

_____

_____

If Jesus truly is who He claimed to be and if Jesus truly did what John says He did, then what are the implications for your life?

_____

_____

_____

_____

_____

_____

_____

_____

_____

_____

DAY 21

John 21.1-25 (NLT)

Jesus appeared to His disciples many times over a 40-day period of time, showing Himself to be very much alive. While John doesn't record every appearance of Jesus, he does add this special story, showing how Jesus forgave Peter's denial and reinstated him as the leader of the new Christian movement. If you have ever done something so bad you think you could never be forgiven, then take encouragement from this story today.

Epilogue: Jesus Appears to Seven Disciples
¹Later, Jesus appeared again to the disciples beside the Sea of Galilee. This is how it happened. ²Several of the disciples were there—Simon Peter, Thomas (nicknamed the Twin), Nathanael from Cana in Galilee, the sons of Zebedee, and two other disciples. ³Simon Peter said, "I'm going fishing."

"We'll come, too," they all said. So they went out in the boat, but they caught nothing all night.

⁴At dawn Jesus was standing on the beach, but the disciples couldn't see who he was. ⁵He called out, "Fellows, have you caught any fish?"

"No," they replied.

⁶Then he said, "Throw out your net on the right-hand side of the boat, and you'll get some!" So they did, and they couldn't haul in the net because there were so many fish in it.

7Then the disciple Jesus loved said to Peter, "It's the Lord!" When Simon Peter heard that it was the Lord, he put on his tunic (for he had stripped for work), jumped into the water, and headed to shore. **8**The others stayed with the boat and pulled the loaded net to the shore, for they were only about a hundred yards from shore. **9**When they got there, they found breakfast waiting for them—fish cooking over a charcoal fire, and some bread.

10"Bring some of the fish you've just caught," Jesus said. **11**So Simon Peter went aboard and dragged the net to the shore. There were 153 large fish, and yet the net hadn't torn.

12"Now come and have some breakfast!" Jesus said. None of the disciples dared to ask him, "Who are you?" They knew it was the Lord. **13**Then Jesus served them the bread and the fish. **14**This was the third time Jesus had appeared to his disciples since he had been raised from the dead.

15After breakfast Jesus asked Simon Peter, "Simon son of John, do you love me more than these?"

"Yes, Lord," Peter replied, "you know I love you."

"Then feed my lambs," Jesus told him.

16Jesus repeated the question: "Simon son of John, do you love me?"

"Yes, Lord," Peter said, "you know I love you."

"Then take care of my sheep," Jesus said.

17A third time he asked him, "Simon son of John, do you love me?" Peter was hurt that Jesus asked the question a third time. He said, "Lord, you know everything. You know that I love you."

Jesus said, "Then feed my sheep.

18 "I tell you the truth, when you were young, you were able to do as you liked; you dressed yourself and went wherever you wanted to go. But when you are old, you will stretch out your hands, and

others will dress you and take you where you don't want to go."
¹⁹Jesus said this to let him know by what kind of death he would glorify God. Then Jesus told him, "Follow me."

²⁰Peter turned around and saw behind them the disciple Jesus loved—the one who had leaned over to Jesus during supper and asked, "Lord, who will betray you?" ²¹Peter asked Jesus, "What about him, Lord?"

²²Jesus replied, "If I want him to remain alive until I return, what is that to you? As for you, follow me." ²³So the rumor spread among the community of believer that this disciple wouldn't die. But that isn't what Jesus said at all. He only said, "If I want him to remain alive until I return, what is that to you?"

²⁴This disciple is the one who testifies to these events and has recorded them here. And we know that his account of these things is accurate.

²⁵Jesus also did many other things. If they were all written down, I suppose the whole world could not contain the books that would be written.

What were the disciples doing when they met Jesus according to verse 3?

_____

_____

_____

_____

_____

_____

_____

How did they recognize Jesus according to verses 6-7?

What did Peter do when he recognized Jesus in verse 7?

What question did Jesus ask Peter three times according to verse 17? Why do you think Jesus asked Peter this question three times?

What did Jesus tell people to do in verses 17 and 19?

What does this encounter tell you about Jesus and how He deals with our failures? _____

_____

_____

_____

_____

_____

Thoughts: _____

_____

_____

_____

_____

_____

_____

_____

_____

_____

_____

_____

_____

_____

_____

_____

_____

CONGRATULATIONS

Y ou have completed the 21-day journey, and you have learned so much about Jesus. You may be asking yourself, **"Now what should I do?"** Remember, John didn't write his account to simply inform you about Jesus; he wrote his account so that you would believe and follow Jesus.

"...these are written so that you may continue to believe that Jesus is the Messiah, the Son of God, and that by believing in him you will have life by the power of his name," **(John 20.31 ESV)**.

The early disciples of Jesus took this message and spread it all over the world. Still today, millions of people from every culture and nationality are hearing the message of Jesus and finding forgiveness, peace and eternal life in His name. Often the message of Jesus is called the "gospel," which means "good news." So, what is the good news about Jesus?

THE PATH

I will never forget climbing my first 14,000-foot peak in Colorado. At the beginning, the path was very clear and obvious. The path seemed worn and gradual as we trekked through the tall pine trees and past mountain meadows. I thought to myself, "This is going to be easy!" But as we started to switchback up the mountain and the grade became steeper, I could tell I was in for a hard day's work. Once we cleared the tree line, the path all but disappeared. Only stacked stones called "cairns" marked the path to the summit. At one point we thought we could see the summit, and left the path for a shortcut up one face of the mountain, only to find that it led to a false summit and some pretty treacherous cliffs. We had to cautiously backtrack several miles to get back on the right path. Ultimately we made it to the top, exhausted but victorious! I learned a life lesson that day that has stayed with me all these years. The path you choose determines your destination. Think about taking a trip. If you live in Dallas and want to take your family to the sunny beaches of San Diego, California, you don't get on Interstate 20 heading east. You might make it to Atlanta, but no matter how well intentioned you may be or how badly you want to be in California, you would never get to San Diego. Why? The path you chose didn't lead there. That day on the mountain, I thought I could take a different path and get to the summit, but I was wrong. In the same way, the path you choose in life determines your destination.

God created you to know Him personally and walk with Him along a path He has for you. The Bible calls this the path of life. *"You make known to me the **path of life**; in your presence there is fullness of joy; at your right hand are pleasures forevermore,"* **(Psalm 16.11 ESV)**.

Along this path you will find *"fullness of joy"* in God's presence and experience all the good things He has for you. At the very beginning of creation, God made all things, and He made them all good **(Genesis 1.31)**. The first people God made enjoyed a perfect relationship with Him. They knew God and experienced His fellowship on a daily basis. God created you with that same goal in mind; to know Him and to fulfill the purpose He has for you.

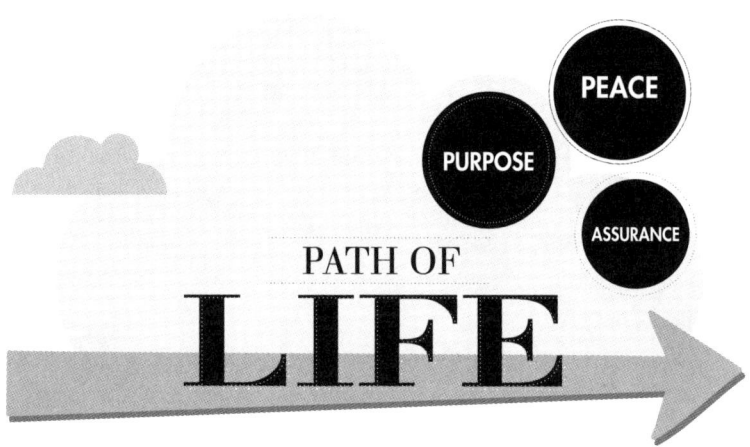

Jesus said, *"And this is the way to have eternal life--to know you, the only true God, and Jesus Christ, the one you sent to earth,"* **(John 17.3 ESV)**. The word "know" doesn't just mean to know facts about something. It means to have an intimate personal knowledge of someone. That's why God created you; to know Him.

Along this path God promises peace, purpose and assurance. Peace means that on this path of life, you find peace with God and the secret to peace with other people. Purpose means that along this path, you will discover who you are and how you can fulfill the purpose God has for your life. And assurance means that along this path, you can know with confidence that you will spend eternity with God in heaven.

THE DETOUR

God created you to know Him and walk with Him along His perfect path, but unfortunately, most people are not experiencing God like that today. Why? Because *something* happened that has diverted us from God's path. That *something* is our own waywardness. Although God has a path that is perfect, we have an innate desire to go our own way, do our own thing, and go off-road from God's path. The prophet Isaiah put it this way, *"All we like sheep have gone astray; we have turned—every one—to his own way,"* **(Isaiah 53.6 ESV)**.

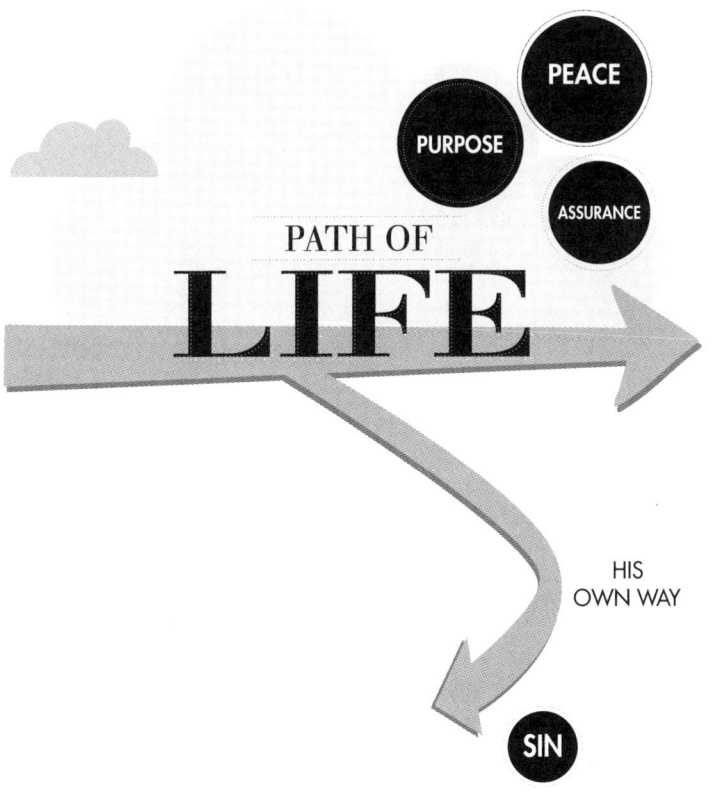

The Bible calls this straying away *"sin."* Sin is disobeying and going against God's direction for our lives. Sin is choosing to live for myself rather than live for the God who created me, knows me and loves me. Originally, sin was an archery term used to describe an archer that missed the bull's-eye, and in our own way, we have each missed the mark of God's created design. We have gone astray. We have taken a turn for the worse. We have left God's path to forge our own way.

The first person God made was Adam. Although Adam knew and walked with God, he chose to disobey Him, and as a result sin came into the world. **(Romans 5.12 NLT)** says, *"When Adam sinned, sin entered the world. Adam's sin brought death, so death spread to everyone, for everyone sinned."* Consequently, all of us now have a selfish and sinful bent to go astray from God. Just like a wheel that's been knocked out of alignment and now pulls to one side, our natural bent is to pull away from God. **(Romans 3.23 NLT)** says, *"For everyone has sinned; we all fall short of God's glorious standard."* Notice the word *"everyone."* That includes you. All of us have chosen to go our own way. Consequently, we live in a world that has lost its way and is headed in the wrong direction, leaving pain and misery in its wake. While following our own path may look good at first, ultimately it only leads to a dead end and isolation from God.

HITTING THE WALL

When you and I make the decision to go our own way, leaving God's path to chart our own, it always results in hitting the wall. Usually this comes in the form of some crisis or difficulty. Sometimes it comes in a quiet feeling of loneliness or desperation. Often it is a quiet sense that we are far from God, and we don't know how to get back. Suddenly, we realize that we are not living out God's intended purpose for our lives. We recognize we don't have peace with God or with people. We acknowledge that we don't have assurance that when we die, we are going to Heaven. It is then that we understand the road we have taken has led to a dead end, and we are isolated from God. The prophet Isaiah wrote: *"[Y]our iniquities [sins] have separated you from your God; your sins have hidden his face from you, so that he will not hear,"* **(Isaiah 59.2 NIV)**. Sin always leads to separation. At some point, you may try to do things to get yourself back on track with God. You may try being a better person, doing good things for people, even becoming more religious, but nothing can change your situation. Again Isaiah wrote: *"We are all infected and impure with sin. When we display our righteous deeds, they are nothing but filthy rags,"* **(Isaiah 64.6 NLT)**. Even your best isn't good enough.

When you turned to go your own way, you turned your back on God. But in His love and kindness, God never turned His back on you. Hitting the wall is actually a good thing, because it awakens you to your desperate need for God. It brings you to the place where you realize how far you've drifted and gives you a chance to make a course correction. If anyone stubbornly continues to go down the wrong road, ultimately that person will hit the wall of God's justice. **(Romans 14.12 NLT)** says, *"Yes, each of us will give a personal account to God. Those who are found guilty of sin and refuse to turn to God will experience God's justice."* **(Nahum 1.3 NLT)** says, *"The Lord is slow to get angry, but his power is great, and he never lets the guilty go unpunished."* Because God is just, He cannot tolerate injustice. Because He is holy, He cannot ignore sin. What is the punishment for sin? **(Romans 6.23 ESV)** begins with these startling words, *"For the wages of sin is death...,"*. The punishment for our sin and waywardness is not just physical death, but spiritual death and separation from God forever. This is the bad news of the Bible. We've lost our way, and we are powerless to get back on our own.

THE CROSS

When there was no hope — and at just the right time — Jesus came into the world, **(Romans 5.6 ESV)**. Though Jesus was by nature fully God, He set aside His eternal glory and was born as a baby **(Philippians 2.6-8 ESV)**. He grew up just like you and me. He experienced temptation and pain, heartache and betrayal. He lived our life, yet He did it without sin. He never veered off course from His heavenly Father's path **(Hebrews 4.15 ESV)**. He lived the life we were meant to live, walking the path of life and enjoying His Father's presence, just as we were designed to do. Because He was perfect in every way, Jesus could now step in as a substitute for you and me, and pay for our sin. In His ultimate act of love, Jesus was crucified and died on a cross for our sin, paying our punishment in full. Think about it. All our sin was rolled onto the back of innocent Jesus, and God the Father treated Him just as if He had sinned our sin, **(2 Corinthians 5.21 ESV)**. He bore your sin and mine on that cross, suffering God's wrath against sin. From the cross Jesus cried out the word, *"tetelestai,"* which means *"it is complete"* or *"paid in full"* **(John 19.30 ESV)**. These were the words a merchant would stamp on a receipt to prove the debt was paid. That is what Jesus did for you. He paid your sin debt in full so you could be forgiven and start over. **(Romans 6.23 ESV)** says, *"For the wages of sin is death, but the free gift*

of God is eternal life in Christ Jesus our Lord." Jesus died on a cross, and His body was buried in a borrowed tomb. Three days later He rose from the dead, conquering sin and death. After His resurrection, He appeared to hundreds of people over a forty-day period, proving Himself to be alive, **(Acts 1.3 ESV)**. **(l Peter 3.18 NLT)** says, *"Christ suffered for our sins once for all time. He never sinned, but he died for sinners to bring you safely home to God."* Jesus did what our own good works could never do – He made a way for us get back to God.

Hearing all that Jesus has done, anyone would wonder, *"Why?"* Why did Jesus do all of this for you and me? One word: love. **(John 3.16 ESV)** says, *"For God so loved the world that he gave his only Son, that whoever believes in him should not perish but have eternal life."* You could scratch out the word "world" and put your name in its place. Think about it. God sent His Son, Jesus, on a rescue mission from Heaven, just for you! That's incredible love. That's an incredible hero.

THE ONLY WAY

On the night before His death, Jesus told His disciples, *"I am the way, the truth, and the life. No one can come to the Father except through me."* **(John 14.6 NLT)**. In this one simple sentence, Jesus made some bold claims. He said *"I am the truth."* Not just that He knew the truth or pointed people to the truth, but that He was the truth of God embodied. All the promises of God and hopes of the people were once and for all wrapped up and fulfilled in Jesus. He said, *"I am the life."* Only Jesus gives life to the fullest here and eternal life in the hereafter. He also claimed, *"I am the way."* The way where? The way back to God. Just as an on-ramp brings you back onto a highway, Jesus is the only way back to God and the path of life He has for you. You may ask, "In a world of so many different religions, why is Jesus the only way?" The simple answer is that there is no one like Jesus. Jesus is the only one who fulfilled hundreds of ancient Jewish prophecies pointing to the coming Messiah. Jesus is the only one who legitimately claimed to be God in the flesh. Jesus is the only one who died for the sins of all people. No religious leader claimed to do such a thing. Jesus is the only one to defeat the grave. Check the graves of the other religious leaders, and you will find their bones, but Jesus' grave is empty. Jesus is also the only one to offer eternal life in His name. Most religions are based on doing good works to earn eternal life, but Jesus offers life based on His finished work on the cross. Jesus stands head and shoulders above the rest.

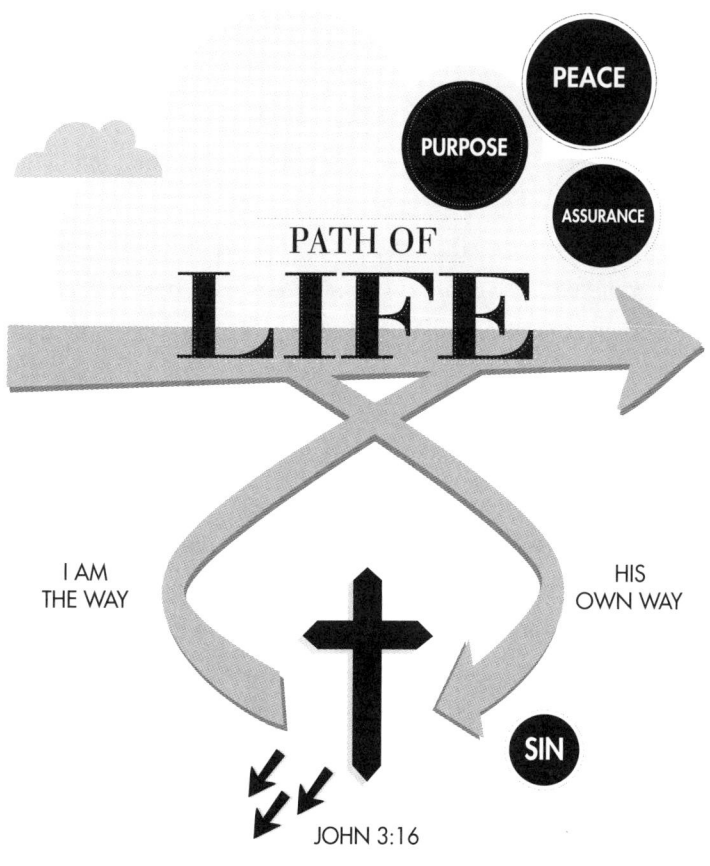

Not only did Jesus claim to be the only way back to God, He also warned that other ways lead to destruction. *"You can enter God's Kingdom only through the narrow gate. The highway to hell is broad, and its gate is wide for the many who choose that way. But the gateway to life is very narrow and the road is difficult, and only a few ever find it,"* **(Matthew 7.13-14 NLT)**. Most people are traveling the "wayward road" that leads away from God. Jesus warned that road is like an eight-lane highway that leads ultimately to destruction. But the "only way" back home is a narrow way, through Jesus alone and only a few choose to walk that road. **(I John 5.12 NLT)** makes it clear: *"Whoever has the Son has life; whoever does not have God's Son does not have life."*

HEADED HOME

Heading home is a choice. While Jesus made a way for you to be right with God, you still must respond to what He has done. How should you respond? Jesus made it very clear in His first recorded sermon. **(Mark 1.15 NIV)** says, *"'The time has come', he said. 'The kingdom of God has come near. Repent and believe the good news!'."* In this short statement Jesus proclaimed that the Kingdom of God and the Promised Messiah had now come.

Now, people are called to respond in two ways. First, Jesus said "repent." Repentance means to simply change your mind and change your direction. A repenting person is aware of their sin and is broken over it. **(Psalm 38.18 NLT)** says, *"But I confess my sins; I am deeply sorry for what I have done. Instead of blaming others, minimizing or excusing, a repentant person is broken over their sin and willingly turns from it."* Repentance also means that you see the direction you are going on that "wayward road," and you make a conscious decision to turn off of it, leaving your old lifestyle behind to follow the leadership of

Jesus and obey Him. You can't follow Jesus and keep going your way. **(I John 2.6 NIV)** says, *"Whoever claims to live in him must live as Jesus did."* Repentance means turning the corner and acknowledging Jesus as the forgiver and leader of your life.

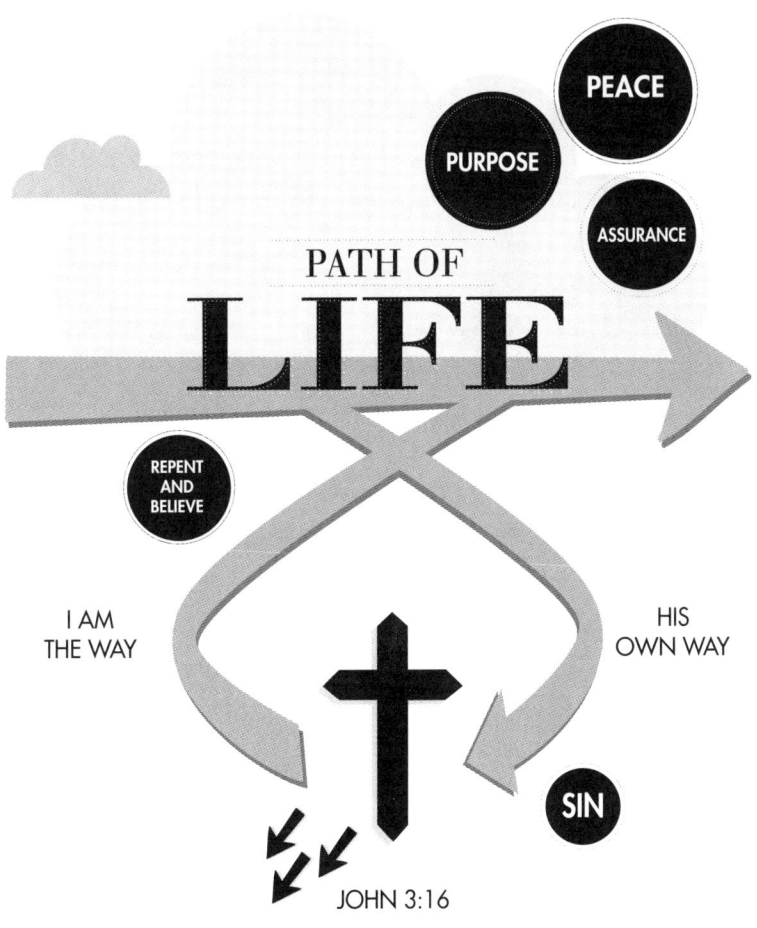

Jesus also said we respond to all He has done by "believing" in Him. To believe in Jesus means to believe that Jesus is who He claimed to be, and that He has done what He claimed to do. It means acknowledging Jesus as the Son of God who died in your place, was buried and rose again in power. Believing also means that you act on what you believe to be true. To believe in Jesus involves a decision to place your trust and hope in Jesus alone for your forgiveness and your eternity. No longer are you trusting in your own efforts, good works or religious practice to save you. You are trusting in Jesus alone and His work on the cross. **Romans 10.9 ESV** states, *"...if you confess with your mouth that Jesus is Lord and believe in your heart that God raised him from the dead, you will be saved."*

Repenting and believing is your response to all Jesus has done for you. You can choose to go your own way, down that broad road, or you can choose to turn to Jesus. It's your choice. To those who choose to follow Jesus, he gives a wonderful promise. *"My sheep listen to my voice; I know them, and they follow me. I give them eternal life, and they will never perish. No one can snatch them away from me, for my Father has given them to me, and he is more powerful than anyone else. No one can snatch them from the Father's hand. The Father and I are one,"* **(John 10.27-30, NLT)**.

Where are you in this diagram? _____
_____
_____
_____
_____
_____
_____
_____
_____
_____

Would you be willing to turn to Christ right now and put your trust in Him?
_____
_____
_____
_____

PRAYER

If you are ready to follow Jesus by repenting and believing in Him, then you can pray a simple prayer like this: Dear Heavenly Father, I know that You have a purpose for my life, but I have sinned against You and have gone my own way. I know I deserve judgment, but I believe that Jesus died for my sin. I believe that He rose from the dead, and I believe that only He can save me. So right now, I am turning from my sin and putting my trust in You. Please forgive me. Lead my life. Make me clean. Give me a home in heaven. I choose today to follow You. Amen.

BACK ON TRACK

Now that you have turned to Jesus and put your trust in Him, you are now on the path where God intended you to be. As you begin to walk with God, let me give you a few things you can do to grow in your relationship with Jesus. First, it is important that you let someone know of the decision you have made. If you have a Christian friend, tell them that you have decided to follow Jesus. They will be thrilled for you, and they can pray for you and encourage you along the way. Second, you can keep reading the Bible. Just as you read through the Gospel of John, there are many other things you can learn about Jesus. So, get a Bible and start reading it. I suggest that you read through the Gospel of Luke. There are many other stories there about Jesus that will encourage you. Third, you need to find a church where you can learn how to walk with God and enjoy the company of other Christ followers. Pick a church that teaches the Bible and will help you grow. Fourth, pray. Talk to God throughout the day. Ask Him to help you and lead you every step you take.

FINAL THOUGHTS

_____
_____
_____
_____
_____
_____
_____
_____